RIDING THE
CROSSROADS

RIDING THE
CROSSROADS

HERBIE SHREVE

WITH DAVID WIMBISH & DAVID HAZARD

CHRISTIAN MOTORCYCLISTS ASSOCIATION
P.O. BOX 9, HATFIELD, ARKANSAS 71945 • (501) 389-6196

This book is
dedicated to the memory of

SHIRLEY SHREVE

"FIRST LADY OF CMA"
1934–1994

FOREWORD

If the apostle Paul were around today, no doubt he would have flown around in a jet.

So much to be done! So many unreached, so many suffering, such great multitudes waiting to hear the best message ever brought to mankind: Our Creator and Father loves us so much, He sent His only Son to die for us. He came down from heaven to find us in all our lost, dark and hurting ways. So often I have shared these amazing truths in meetings where I try to convince Christians that time is short, needs are horrendous and workers are few.

Herb and Herbie Shreve, and the members of the Christian Motorcyclists Association, are answering the cries of men and women who need the one true message of hope. A motorcycle can take you to places where many people need to hear the good news—to rallies, campouts, and bike shops. And being close to people is such an important part of sharing the message of Jesus Christ, who Himself came to be close to us all.

Again, the apostle Paul said he would do anything to reach and save even a few. And because he had such a generous, self-sacrificing heart, he reached many for Christ. In their willingness to go and do likewise, the Shreves and the members of CMA have been a tremendous blessing to many—including my organization, Open Doors, and me personally.

As you read this book, keep in mind that it is more than the story of a father and son. It's a living record of the Lord's work in people who are committed to a vision—God's vision of reaching a lost world. Every Christian should read this story.

To all the members of CMA I want to say—you're on the right track! Keep in high-gear and never stop until you get there . . . wherever Jesus sends you. Don't even stop for a red light—that is, not if that "red light" is some devil-inspired or man-made barrier. Never stop sharing the gospel!

Gladly your companion,

Brother Andrew
Founder, Open Doors
The Netherlands

Lost in America

He clenched his fist. For a moment I thought he was going to hit me. His eyes flashed with anger.

"Listen," he growled. "I don't want to hear anymore. Do you understand? I'm not interested in *your* Jesus!"

I was in a roadside rest area along I-40 in Tennessee, somewhere between Memphis and Nashville. I'd stopped to see if I could help a young man who was obviously having trouble with his motorcycle. He was somewhere between 25 and 30, dressed in jeans, leathers, and wore the patch of a well-known biker group. We had been having a pleasant conversation—until I mentioned Jesus, and that's when the smoke started coming out of his ears.

I'd seen that reaction before.

In fact, there had been a time when I had felt exactly the same way.

"I didn't mean to make you mad," I said. "I just wanted you to know that Jesus loves you."

He snorted and bent down to pick up a wrench.

"Yeah, sure . . . Jesus loves me."

He stood up and waved the wrench in my face.

"You know . . . I've seen some of your Christian friends on television, driving limousines, living in mansions that their viewers paid for and fleecing the flock every chance they get."

I shook my head, "That has nothing to do with it."

"It has plenty to do with it. Jesus . . . He may look out for the rich . . . but He doesn't care about a poor boy like me.

"If Jesus loves me, let Him come down here and show me. Let Him help me find a job. Let Him help me get my old lady to come back to me . . . or at least let me see my little girl. Let Him get my old man to tell me, for once in his life, that he's proud of me. No . . . I don't see your Jesus stooping down to show me how much He loves me." He laughed sarcastically. "Let Him help me fix my bike if He loves me so much."

I reached out and gently put my hand on his shoulder.

"But that's exactly why I'm here."

That startled him. The angry look softened ever so slightly. Then he turned away. "Aw, what would you know about it?"

I smiled. "I know plenty. I've been there. I know exactly how you feel."

He shrugged, bent over his bike, and gave a few more twists with the wrench.

"Lord," I prayed silently, "help me. Give me something to say to this guy. Help me make him understand how much you love him."

My mind went back to another time—more than 20 years ago—to another angry young man. It was difficult, looking back, to realize that angry, rebellious, troubled young man had been me.

CHAPTER 1

The Rebel

Dad was home again. I could hear him calling to my mother as he came in and sat his suitcase down.

"Shirley? I'm home."

"Herbie, I'm here."

Big deal.

That's what I thought about it.

He'd be home for a few days, just long enough to make another one of his attempts to get me to "toe the line." Then he'd leave again. Out there, in those nice churches full of nice people, he would preach about the love of God. He spent so much time worrying about the souls of nameless people. As far as I was concerned, he should have spent a little less time worrying about the spiritual condition of rural Arkansas and more time worrying about the welfare of his own family. And about me, his own son. His namesake.

My attitude wasn't completely fair. But it did seem that Dad was away during almost every important occasion of my life. By the time I hit my early teens, I had very little use for the man. And no use at all for the gospel he preached, or for his God.

I sat in the living room, staring dull-eyed at the TV, listening as Dad opened the refrigerator in search of a cola.

"Herbie?" he called again.

I was full of anger and resentment, and my icy silence would let him know it.

Now I heard Mom's voice.

"Herbie? Did you . . ."

She was always checking to see if I'd done all the chores I was supposed to do in Dad's absence.

Right.

Take out the garbage. Clean the garage. Sure, other kids had chores. But I somehow thought too much was left to me, so Dad could go away and "do the Lord's work."

Mom found me in the living room, and asked me if I'd done something or other. I don't remember now what it was, but I do remember that Dad came into the room right behind her and heard my smart-alecky response. When he did, his face went red.

"Don't talk to your mother that way," he barked. "You tell her right now that you're sorry."

Oh, perfect. He'd been gone for days. Now he walks in and becomes "the general." At 16, I was through taking orders.

Without so much as acknowledging his existence, I got up and walked out of the room, my shoulder bumping his as I went by. In my room, I flopped down on my bed and picked up the guitar. Dad followed right behind me.

"I'm not playing games with you, Herbie," he said. "You tell your mother you're sorry."

Instead of answering, I plucked at the strings—loud, shrill notes that were meant to mock his voice.

He stood glowering down at me, insisting again that I "had" to apologize. I just kept plucking those squeaky, mocking notes. He was a joke. Everything was a joke.

When I'd hit 6'2" in the seventh grade, I'd gotten too big for Mother to control. I did what I pleased while Dad was away. But when he came home, things changed drastically Then it was, "Yes, sir," this and "No, sir," that. But this time

I'd had enough of that sort of thing. It was time I taught him who was really in charge here.

That was the moment Dad reached down and grabbed the neck of my guitar. Ripping it from my hands, he tossed it into the corner.

I jumped to my feet, swinging. The first blow caught my father on the chin and he staggered. The look of shock— the anguish—gave me a surge of bitter satisfaction. I had figured one punch would lay him out. But in the next second, he took a swing that hammered me hard on the jaw.

A second later, I was on my back looking up at the ceiling.

The old man was a lot stronger than I'd figured.

I got on my feet again. Mom was in the doorway. Lunging, I tried to hit Dad again. He jumped out of the way and I missed completely. This time he grabbed my arm. While Mom screamed for us to stop, I wrestled furiously, but he had my arm behind me as we banged our way out of my bedroom, through the living room where the TV was mindlessly babbling. We crashed through the screen door and out onto the porch.

Somehow my knees buckled and Dad was on top of me, pinning me to the deck. I was sweating. Cursing. Pushing. But I couldn't budge.

"I don't want to fight you, Herbie," he said, gasping. "But I'm not going to put up with this. *Do you understand me?*"

I struggled to get loose, but the man's fingers were like iron, digging painfully into my arms.

"Do you understand me?" he bellowed.

I refused to give him the satisfaction of an answer.

Holding me in a half-nelson, he jerked me to my feet— pushing me down the steps, he propelled me toward his car, which was parked in the driveway. I struggled and resisted all the way. My arms and neck were aching. And then I tasted blood on my lip. I kept trying to get free, but the man's strength was unbelievable. I'd been in quite a few fights by this time, and thought I was tough. But I'd never gone up against strength like this.

Still pinning one arm behind my back, he managed to open the passenger side door and push me into the seat.

"Now, you just *sit* there," he barked.

I was seething. But grudgingly I sat there as he walked around and climbed into the driver's seat.

When he backed out of the driveway, he gunned it, spewing gravel as we shot out into the street. I could feel his anger as his hands clenched the wheel in that iron grip.

I didn't know where we were going, but I wasn't about to object. I was whipped—this time, at least. For now, I figured the best thing to do was to sit there and keep my mouth shut.

We drove a good 10 or 15 miles away—far out into the woods outside of town. Dad rivetted his eyes to the road the entire time. Sullenly, I nursed my bruised jaw and my more seriously injured ego. The hills and woods of Arkansas flashed by—but all I could see were the angry memories. All the hundreds of times I had to sit quietly on a hard wooden pew, while Dad stood up there in the pulpit, high and mighty and gushing about God's love. Spouting righteous words from the Bible. All Dad ever did was talk about God . . . some big man in the sky who seemed to me as remote as my own father. God was not real to me. If God *was* real, why didn't He show up in the real, gritty world right here in rural Arkansas? Why were we all supposed to go where He was—if He really was in those nice, clean churches . . . which I doubted. If God was this loving Father Dad talked about, swinging his black Bible in front of everyone, then why didn't He come right down into my world and let me *know* He was real? If God was God, he could do that, right? Or was He just too good to get close to an angry kid like me?

I wanted Dad and all his God-talk to go away and leave me alone.

Finally, Dad pulled over in a remote turn-around area in a grove of pine trees.

"This is it," I thought. "He's gonna kill me."

No, that was stupid. More likely, he was going to tell me to get out and not come back. Maybe he wanted me out of his house and his life as much as I wanted him off my back.

Outside, a bird called. Otherwise, it was silent.

Suddenly, Dad leaned forward, resting his head on the steering wheel. His chest heaved, and he began to weep. Great racking sobs came out of this powerful man.

I was surprised. Embarrassed. Dad just hung his head there on the steering wheel and sobbed.

"What am I going to do with you?" he cried. "What in the world am I going to do with you?"

Dad was going to have to do more than blubber. A few tears, and I was supposed to open my heart and soul to him again—is that what he thought? No way. My heart was closed. Dad was an effective preacher, and his words moved people. But not me. He'd have to go a long way to get to me now. I had him right where I wanted him . . . crying like a baby.

Dad's sobs had stopped now, but still his forehead rested on his arms, which remained folded across the steering wheel. What was he thinking? Mercifully, he didn't say another word and, in a minute, he started the car again, and began to drive us back home.

I looked out the window, a smirk playing across my lips. But at the same time, I felt just a flicker of another feeling. Just a twinge. *I wanted him to prove he cared about me.*

Quickly, I brushed it aside. No way. I'd shut him out of my life . . . him and his God. And they could stay out.

But it was as if a door had been opened, just a crack. I couldn't have known that my angry thought was my first real honest-to-goodness prayer. And a chain of events would soon be in motion, changing the course of my life, and Dad's forever.

CHAPTER 2

Seeds of Rebellion

As a teenager you know it all—especially what's wrong with adults.

Lots of men make big mistakes with their sons and daughters.

In the weeks that followed my blow-up with Dad, I thought about the men I knew who were real jerks. Oh, sure, some were real nice when they were with their drinking buddies, for instance. But at home they were big-time abusers. They drove their own kids away through their bullying behavior. I knew a number of situations like that right around our town of Hatfield.

Then there were other men—some of them in our own church—who made the mistake of wanting their kids to be perfect. They wanted angels, not children. No matter what their kids tried to do, it was never enough to win their praise and approval.

Dad was not abusive. He was never mean to me.

But for a long, long time, he'd been caught up in his "work for God," and he wasn't there for Mom and me. Not that we didn't have some good times when I was much younger. When I was little, in fact, we'd had a pretty good thing going . . . and it had to do with horses.

My father had always loved horses, and at a very early age he instilled in me a love for riding. We both had horses that we trained and showed. Dad was good with horses and he spent hours teaching me how to be gentle . . . but firm in your control of an animal. His mastery and patience with horses amazed me.

Somehow, his confidence with these large, powerful beasts got into my blood, too. On a particular spring day, I had climbed into the saddle, taken the reins in hand and nudged the horse into a trot. A cool breeze was blowing the scent of fresh rain my way. That's when it happened, I think. That's when the hunger for this rush-feeling of freedom swept inside me. The horse felt powerful beneath me —a power I could control! I felt my chest swell with exhilaration. I made the horse go faster. How could you want anything else but the freedom of a good ride? What else was there? And it was Dad's gift to me.

On the other hand, though, Dad could be so short-sighted about certain things. Important things—like pain.

I was about 10 when Dad and I were working to break a new horse. This animal was mean. He didn't want anybody on his back. Especially some little boy.

No sooner had Dad set me up in the saddle than I went flying off and smacked hard on the ground. Everything went black, and I gasped to get some air into my lungs. My chest ached.

Before I had a chance to catch my breath, Dad picked me up and put me back on the horse. In a heartbeat, with one buck, the horse slammed me to the ground again. Twice, in only a few moments, I had the wind knocked out of me.

To my amazement, Dad seized me and shoved me into the saddle. Couldn't he see I was nearly choking? Sure, he always said he wanted me to be tough, but . . .

In another second, I was airborne again. This time I hit the board fence before landing on the hard dirt. My elbows were bleeding. I couldn't get out a whisper, let alone a yell for help.

Again and again, Dad kept shoving me onto that wild and mean horse. *Slam.* Down I'd go. One knee was cut. My lip smacked into a rock. Couldn't this guy see he was killing me? One time I just lay there and pretended to be dead. It didn't work. I thought Dad wouldn't quit until I *was* dead.

Meanwhile, the man who lived next door had seen the episode. To my relief, he finally rushed over.

"Preacher . . . *please!* You're going to have to let that boy go, or you're going to kill him and me, both!"

Thankfully, my father listened to the man's better judgement.

From Dad's perspective—so he told me later—he was teaching me some important lessons. You have to overcome your fear by learning how to get up and keep going. But I also learned that Dad seemed totally indifferent to me as a human being. That horse was killing me, and he didn't even seem to care.

As I sat in my room that night, I began to wonder. What did Dad think of me? For all the fun we had with horses . . . most of the time . . . horses were his thing. It was great to be included, but it seemed like there was a big gulf between us. Had it always been there? Didn't he like being around me?

True, some circumstances had made it hard for Dad to give me a lot of himself. Several years before, Mom had been diagnosed with cancer of the liver. For two years, she was in and out of the hospital, going steadily downhill. I knew she was dying.

Dad had to scramble to pay the huge medical bills. He preached wherever he could. He taught school. When he wasn't working, he was at the hospital visiting Mom.

I was squeezed out. Of necessity, I spent a lot of time with Mom's parents—who I called Donk and Papaw. They were great people, and I loved them. But at night, I laid in bed and thought about Mom—so gray-looking, so sick and full of pain. "God, heal my mom," I prayed, lying there in the dark.

Dad was consumed by life. We didn't talk much. I know that he also prayed for Mom, and so did several members of his church. But as the months dragged on, it was bleak.

Suddenly, miraculously, Mom's cancer disappeared. The pink of health flushed her pale skin again. Strength returned. She was healed.

Doctors were thrown at first, and so they did one test after another. In the end, they satisfied themselves by calling it a "spontaneous remission."

Within a month, Mom was home from the hospital for good. When she walked in the front door, she turned to Dad—and there they stood, holding each other, crying and laughing at the same time. That Sunday, when she walked into church under her own strength, a few of those staid Baptists let loose with some hearty shouts of "Praise the Lord!" Everyone was awed that God had "touched" my mother.

Her healing was a two-edged sword for me. Maybe it was just that I was so young, but all the talk about God and miracles went right by me. I was just happy to have Mom back. The downside was that I lost Dad more than ever. Over the next few years, he began to pastor several different churches in and around Hatfield. Because the congregations were small and couldn't really afford to support a pastor, Dad continued teaching. And when he wasn't at church or at school, his first love was evangelism. He loved to hit the road to preach the "good news of salvation through Jesus Christ." Every chance that came along, he took it. And every time he left home, I felt that same sense of abandonment and loneliness. The time we spent with the horses had some good moments—but it was also a lot of hard work. Even before the "killer horse" incident, I'd begun to resent Dad for living a life so distant from mine.

Just before I turned 12, we moved to El Dorado, Arkansas. Things were good there because the church was a bit bigger, and that meant two things were different.

First, Dad was making more money. He no longer had to supplement his income by teaching school. Second, there were more calls for the pastor during the week—which meant he couldn't be gone so much of the time. The schedule did fill in though—what with attending five or six committee meetings every week. And then he had to visit the sick and the "backslidden." There wasn't much time to travel out of town on evangelistic trips—but there wasn't much time for the family either.

I sure wanted things to change. As we settled in El Dorado, I imagined Dad would have more time to spend with me. I pictured us going on long horseback rides together. Maybe we could even become "pals." And maybe Dad would be home more, I thought, after the adoption of my new baby brother, Kelly.

But our lives were about to be thrown into more turmoil.

It all began innocently enough. Late one Saturday evening, I was working on my Sunday School lesson for the next day. Dad was sitting at the kitchen table, going over notes for his sermon.

"Dad," I called to him. "What's an allegory?"

"An allegory? It's kind of . . . like . . . a fable. Or a myth."

"Oh."

I scribbled an answer in my workbook and went on reading. But in a moment, Dad was standing at my door. "Why'd you ask me that? Where'd you hear the word allegory anyway?"

I shrugged. "It says right here in this lesson book that the story of Jonah is an allegory."

"*What?* What in the world are you reading?"

I started to answer, "It's just my Sunday School . . . ," but before I could get the words out, he strode across the room and snatched the book out of my hand.

"You mean *this* book says the story of Jonah isn't true?"

"Uh-huh."

Dad got the strangest look on his face. Something like anger, hurt, or shock.

He continued to flip through the lesson to see what else it had to say. By his own count, he found something like 15 instances where this book, aimed at junior-high-school age boys and girls, directly challenged the truth of the Bible. And it was put out by our own denomination!

By the time Dad finished reading, only one emotion showed on his face. Anger. By now, Mom had come in, having settled Kelly for the night.

"What's wrong?"

"When the people at church hear about this—this garbage—they won't stand for it either!" Dad replied, waving the offending book in Mom's face. After all, this was Arkansas—the middle of the Bible Belt. People believed in the Holy Scriptures, and they were ready and willing to defend them.

The next day, though, very few people were as stirred up as Dad. Then, he called some fellow preachers. "Now simmer down, Herb," one of them said. "You don't want to get a reputation as a troublemaker."

"Leave it alone," another pastor told him. "It's not worth fighting about."

These guys didn't know Dad. When God's honor and God's Word were at stake, nothing else mattered.

Dad drew up a petition. With a raft of signatures, he

marched into the denominational convention. This would help the church see it needed to change its Sunday school materials.

A few days later, Dad arrived at home with a triumphant smile. "They sure got an ear full from me," he told Mom. "I think they got the message."

Not ten minutes had passed before the phone rang. One of the church members was calling to let Dad in on a secret. There was going to be a special meeting at our church that night. He needed to be there.

The church was packed that evening. To Dad's astonishment, most of the executive committee denounced him as a stubborn, angry man who would not listen to his superiors or reason. "You're only trying to stir up trouble for your own purposes," he was told.

I know it was an awful experience for Dad, because it was absolutely brutal for me, watching and listening as he was verbally torn apart. One after another, six men I had respected and admired rose to challenge and ridicule my father—men like my Sunday School teacher, a deacon or two, my friends' fathers, etc.

How could they sit there and say such terrible things about this good man? How could God let them do this to him? I hated them for what they were doing. I hated Dad for not fighting back. And I questioned God for allowing it to happen.

As I watched, from the sidelines, I could feel my heart pounding in my throat. My face felt like it was on fire. I was overwhelmed by hatred. All I could think of was revenge. I would get even with those men for this. Oh, yes. I would make them pay.

This was supposed to be a "fair and impartial" meeting, but it was nothing of the sort. It was a well-planned, efficiently carried out execution.

When the meeting ended, the church had run Dad out. He was fired. Period. We had two weeks to pack and move out of the parsonage. I felt so humiliated.

When I walked out into the dark, I looked up at the black night sky, thinking, "That's it. If this is what happens when you serve God, then who needs Him?" On the way home, I began to build a head of steam. I wondered if there even *was* a God? As soon as I was old enough to get out on my own, that would be it. No more church. No more God-talk.

A small group of supporters followed us home, and while they sat in the living room consoling my parents, I went off on my own. I slammed the door of my bedroom and flung myself down on my bed. Hot tears of anger stung my eyes.

I hated those six men so much for what they'd done to Dad—to all of us.

Out of the corner of my eye, I saw something standing in the corner of my closet. A baseball bat—an *equalizer*.

I went and picked it up, whacking the bed as hard as I could.

And then, in a frenzy, I did it again . . . and again and again. I could see myself cracking a few heads open. Yes, that's what I should do.

I stormed out into the living room, gripping the bat tightly in both hands and—I'm sure—with murder written on my face.

Dad leaped from his chair. "What's going on, Son?"

I charged toward the door. He blocked my way.

"I'm gonna hurt them," I said, choking on angry tears.

"No." Dad seized me by the arms. I shook him off.

"I'm gonna *kill* them!" I shouted it. "I'm gonna smash their heads in!"

"No, you're not!" Dad went for the bat, and I pulled it away.

"Let me go!"

I tried to make a break for it. But Dad and another guy grabbed me. I kicked and screamed as they carried me back into my room, heaving me onto the bed, they locked me inside. I lunged for the door, pounding and screaming. A wild rush of anger took over. "Let me out! Let me out! I'm gonna kill 'em! I'm gonna kill 'em!"

Banging and kicking with all of my might, I began to weep uncontrollably.

How long this went on, I don't know. Fifteen minutes. Twenty minutes. I went on and on until I finally fell to the floor in an exhausted heap.

I was still on the floor when I woke up the next morning. The night's sleep had given me a chance to think twice about going on a head-bashing rampage with a baseball bat. But it had not dimmed my anger at the way Dad had been treated.

In my heart, then and there, I decided if God could turn His back on us, I'd turn my back on Him. I didn't need "nice church" people. Mom and Dad could hold on to their empty faith if they wanted to, but not me.

"Maybe the doctors were right about Mom," I thought angrily. "Maybe her so-called healing has a natural explanation." At the very best, God was too unpredictable—answering a prayer here, ignoring you there. How could I understand a God who acted so whimsically?

I wanted nothing to do with God anymore.

And with that decision, I set myself on a dangerous course.

CHAPTER 3

The Downward Spiral

For the next several years, my life centered around the "wild crowd." Our idea of a good time was beer and loud music. And wheels.

It was no secret that I had always loved motorcycles. When I was in the third grade, my parents had bought me a little Briggs & Stratton mini bike, and I had blown the thing up three times racing it. It was the fastest thing in the area, and I was so proud of it.

Then, when I was about 10, Dad and I had gone to a motorcycle shop just to look at them. I saw a Honda Dream there that almost caused me to start drooling. That bike was appropriately named, because for weeks after that, I rode that Honda every night in my dreams.

And then there had been that wonderful television show about a guy who rode a motorcycle, *Along Came Bronson*. I wouldn't miss it. Even when we had lived in El Dorado, my friends and I had souped up our bikes by sticking baseball cards into the spokes. And then, with our "engines" roaring, we had raced up and down as the "Julia Street Gang."

But El Dorado was long ago, now. That was where *they* lived—the men I hated so much.

After we left there, we came back to the Hatfield area, where Mom's folks were, and Dad went into full-time evangelism. He was gone more now than ever before.

He was hardly ever home, and all the time, the gap between his world and mine grew wider. And, of course, so did the gap between Dad and me. His life was evangelism. Mine was running with the party crowd. There was no way our two worlds could ever meet—and I didn't want them to.

A few days after I'd goaded him into fighting me, he had to go back on the road for another series of evangelistic crusades—back among those "good" people.

Dad was heartbroken about the way things were between us and it showed in the pained look on his face whenever I spoke to him—always with a cold, surly edge to my voice. An uneasy truce reigned, and I could sense Dad would have preferred to stay home to try to work things out with me. But, at the same time, he was compelled to go. The lost were out there, and his drive was to tell them about Jesus. He *had* to go. What a disappointment—to have your oldest son curl his lip in disgust at your life's work.

Here was the biggest slap of all—my father came from a family of preachers. His father was a preacher. His brothers were preachers. Most of his nephews were preachers, too. No doubt, he expected me to fall in line.

He didn't have a clue what to do about me.

Later, I learned that something happened the day Dad left for his latest preaching tour. He was driving down the road when he felt this overwhelming "tug" in his heart. As if God was trying to get his attention. Suddenly, he sensed that if he prayed, God was waiting to show him a way to bridge the gap between us. He began to pray. The answer didn't come that day . . . but it would come—in an unexpected moment . . . a few days later.

Meanwhile, I'd turned a corner. Dad would be gone for much of the next couple of months.

I decided it was time to cut loose and really live my life my way. For one thing, I idolized men who were tough—guys who were too tough to be hurt by anyone or anything. Guys who rode bikes, who kicked butt, and who never backed away from a fight. I didn't see any of those guys in church. What I really wanted was to be an outlaw biker. If I could only ride with a major outlaw pack—man, what a life!

I ran with boys who were much older, and I bluffed my way into a reputation as something of a tough guy. Basically, I had the ability to "stare down" people—to look right through them, as if they weren't there. It didn't matter how frightened I felt, or how much I was shaking on the inside, if a bad guy challenged me in some way, I'd give him that look and he'd almost always back down. Some of the guys I stared down would probably have killed me if I had fought them, but thankfully, I rarely had to fight.

Of course, Dad always came home and laid down "the law." And he was strict. No card-playing. No dances. No movies.

But when he was away, I drank and smoked dope. Mom could holler all she wanted, but she couldn't make me do anything I didn't want to do.

One time I came in so wasted that I staggered past her and fell into bed. I couldn't even get up to go to the bathroom. Instead, I decided just to go out my bedroom window. Somehow, I managed to fall out the window and land in the bushes.

Another time, my little brother Kelly came into my room, got into one of my drawers and pulled out two handfuls of drugs. Mom was angry, but I smooth-talked her, saying that it was stuff I was given but that I really wasn't using it. She kept it from Dad, *good thing*.

Not that I was a complete hell-raiser. I dreamed about

being an outlaw—but I never really got that far. In some ways, I worked hard at being a long-haired rebel, but in other ways I was a run-of-the mill teenager. And a hard-working one at that. I worked after school and on weekends in a neighborhood grocery store. The man who owned the store loved me and treated me like a son. All in all, I was a pretty average kid.

Except for the way I looked at life, through a haze of anger.

I smoked dope—but so did lots of people.

I drank, but so did everybody I hung out with.

I fought, swore, and partied.

Mostly, I got a big thrill from trying to discredit Dad's ministry. If he didn't think enough of me to be a part of my life, I could get back at him by trashing his reputation.

One of my favorite "slaps" at Dad was to drive his car across the Arkansas/Oklahoma line to buy beer. I'd leave it parked right in front of the liquor store, hoping other people would recognize it. I thought it was really funny to park so that the "Jesus Is The Answer" bumper sticker was easily seen from the highway.

Sometimes, people who knew Dad would come up and innocently ask me if I was going to follow in his footsteps and become a preacher. I'd always look at them as if they were crazy and yell, "H— no!"

I loved the shocked look. It was a way to slap the whole world of nice Christians in the face.

Meanwhile, Dad was out on the road, still praying for a way to bring us together.

It was a cool, autumn day in September of 1972. Dad was driving down a lonely stretch of highway in rural Arkansas, when a group of bikers passed him going the opposite direction. He was thinking about me. Wondering what to do. Praying.

He barely noticed the bikers as they sped past. But suddenly, it seemed as if the image was burned into his brain. Motorcycles? Was God saying something about motorcycles? Could that be the answer he had been looking for? In his mind's eye, he saw an image of a father and son riding motorcycles together. They were enjoying one another's company. Learning to be friends again. Finding a common ground.

Dad shifted uncomfortably in his car seat. He was a preacher. People expected him to have a certain dignity. What would people think if they saw him on a motorcycle? But still, if God was in it, and if it was a way he could get close to his son . . . ?

It wasn't but a day or two after that, on a Saturday night, that a friend had asked me to drive him over to Oklahoma to see his girlfriend. When we left, I told my mother that we'd "probably" be home later that evening. But instead, we wound up spending the night at the girl's house, and drove back to my house early on Sunday morning.

As we turned the corner on the street where we lived, I saw something I didn't want to see—my father's car sitting in the driveway.

"Oh, no!"

"What's wrong?" my friend wanted to know.

"My dad's home . . . that's what's wrong. What's *he* doing here? He's not supposed to be home for *weeks* yet."

"So you're gonna catch it, huh?"

I laughed a little uneasily. "No, I'm already caught."

I sighed deeply as I got out of his car, slammed the door, and tried to prepare myself for battle as I walked into the house.

I figured he'd probably jump all over me as soon as I walked through the door.

He was in the kitchen with my mother. I didn't look at him.

"So . . . how's it going, Herbie?" Dad offered

What did he mean by that? I was expecting something more like, "Where in the world have you been?" Or "How dare you worry your mother by staying out all night, like this?"

I shrugged. "It's swell, Dad—things are *swell*," I mumbled. Dad didn't seem to notice my disrespectful behavior.

"You know what I've been thinking?" he went on.

I shrugged again.

"I've been thinking that we should get us a couple of motorcycles."

That got a laugh out of me. "Yeah, sure. That's a great idea." But was he serious?

"Look, Herbie," he said. "I know that the last few years have been hard on us. I haven't been here for you as much as I'd have liked.

"I also know you understand that God has called me to be an evangelist—and that I believe telling people about Jesus is the most important thing anyone can do."

I shrugged.

"But still . . . I wish I could have been here for you more." He went on to tell me that he had been looking for a way to "make it up" to me. And that maybe riding motorcycles together was a beginning. At least we could take a trip together. Get to know each other all over again. Become friends again.

The motorcycle sounded like a great idea to me. The "friends" part? Well . . . .

There were a few stipulations. The biggest one was that I had to pay for half of my own motorcycle. No problem. I could raise the money by selling my horse—the last one

I had—and by saving the money I made at my part-time job.

I never stopped to think about where Dad was going to get the rest of the money for the bikes. We scraped along from week to week. Mom and Dad said, "The Lord always provides," but in my view it was Mom selling Tupperware that helped Him along.

Laying out the cash for a couple of motorcycles was no simple matter for Dad. That's what impressed me—that he was ready to put some money where his mouth was. That he was putting himself into some debt for me.

At least it got my attention.

As we talked about the kind of cycle I wanted, I began to realize this venture certainly wasn't anything he was doing for himself. As much as I had always loved motorcycles, he had disliked them. In fact, as far as I know, he had only been on a motorcycle once in his life, and that hadn't been the best experience. During one of his evangelistic crusades, he had borrowed a motorcycle from a friend, only to wind up taking a spill, ripping his best suit, and ending up with a severe case of "road rash."

But even though his past connection with motorcycling had been far less than pleasant, he was willing to do whatever it took to rebuild our relationship. At the time, though, it was a passing thought. Here one day and gone the next. All I knew was that I was getting my own motorcycle. If Dad was helping me buy a motorcycle because he felt guilty—great. I wasn't going to do anything to make him feel *less* guilty!

My horse sold almost immediately. In fact, I sold him to the very first person who called, for a very good price. Somehow, Dad managed to get the local bank to help him, putting himself in debt.

Within the week, he and I were standing in a motorcycle

shop 100 miles away in Fort Smith. It might as well have been heaven. All that beautiful chrome and leather! All that power!

We wound up buying two Honda 450s, loaded them in the truck we had borrowed from a neighbor, and headed out on the long trek back to Hatfield.

It was raining when we got home, so we put our new motorcycles in my grandmother's garage.

That afternoon was Dad's moment of truth.

I watched as he approached the motorcycle, far more nervous than he had ever been on a horse. I had seen the man climb up on the meanest bucking bronc in the area and never give it a second thought. But he looked at his brand new bike as if it might be infused with the spirit of a Brahma bull.

With the bike standing on its center-stand, he perched nervously in the seat. I showed him where all the gears were, how to use the clutch, and so on. Then I went out and rode around in the rain.

At school my friends couldn't believe that my dad—the preacher—had suddenly gone out and bought a couple of Honda 450s.

"What's going on?" one of them asked. "Is your dad having a mid-life crisis or something?"

"Beats me. Maybe so."

"Well . . . if he is . . . I sure wish my dad would have one!"

To Dad's credit, he overcame his nervousness very quickly. Within a couple of days, he was riding all over the streets of the Mena/Hatfield area. A bit wobbly at first. But he was determined to learn, and it wasn't long before he was riding real well. This was the crazy part. He actually seemed to be enjoying himself.

Within a month after bringing the bikes home, he asked

me if I'd like to go with him to a biker rally in Austin, just to see what it was like.

"Sure. Why not."

We had no idea what awaited us there. But life was about to change . . . for both of us.

CHAPTER 4

Let There Be Motorcycles

Being out on the open highway was one of the most exciting things I had ever experienced.

Talk about exhilarating!

With the wind whipping all around me—even through me, it seemed—the sun beating down, and the green forests of east Texas flashing past.

Looking across at Dad as the landscape flashed by us, I could hardly believe this was the same man I'd known all my life. Herb Shreve had always been one of the most conservative men I knew. One time he'd come home from a church convention upset with some of his colleagues because they had worn *colored* dress shirts. Anything other than a white shirt, a tie and a suit jacket just wouldn't do.

And yet, there he was, dressed in jeans, leathers and boots, barreling down the highway on a motorcycle.

Looking over at him, I thought he really *looked* like a biker. Still, I knew that was the old Herb Shreve underneath, and I wondered what would happen when we got to the rally. Certainly there'd be drinking. Probably some marijuana smoke hanging in the air. Women in tank tops and skimpy shorts. I was afraid that Dad would explode in self-righteous anger, and that would be the end of our motorcycle days.

We turned off the main highway and onto the narrow country road that led into the woods. I could smell woodsmoke from campfires. And as we got closer, I could hear the pulse of heavy rock'n'roll blasting from somebody's van. My heart was racing. I wanted to look cool—like I'd been doing this all my life. Would they accept us? What if Dad started "evangelizing?" We could get pulverized, or laughed out of town.

We rounded a curve in the road, and hundreds of bikes were spread out before us, Harleys, Hondas, Suzukis, you name it—motorcycles of all shapes and sizes, customized in all sorts of ways, chrome glistening in the rays of the early morning sun.

The sound of rock music mingled with the roar of motorcycle engines. The smoke from dozens of campfires and cookstoves rose into the horizon.

Everywhere I looked, there were guys and girls in leathers and boots. There were the colors from a half-dozen different biker groups.

We parked our bikes—and in just a few minutes people came around to invite us to come have burgers, beer, chips, a seat by their fire. I was amazed at how quickly we were accepted—like we were part of a family. Someone took us to a great spot where we could set up our tent. As we unpacked our bedrolls, more people came over to welcome us to the rally.

And that's when a very strange thing started happening.

Now, Dad didn't look the least bit like a preacher. He wasn't wearing a cross. He wasn't carrying a Bible. He wasn't sporting a clerical collar. There was nothing at all to distinguish him from any of the other hundreds of bikers at the rally.

But for some reason, people seemed to want to open up their hearts to him, to pour out all their troubles.

One guy, named Les, offered my dad a beer, which he politely declined.

"Don't blame you," said Les. "This stuff rots your guts. In fact . . . ," he suddenly choked up, ". . . my old lady took my kid and left me. Lord, I love that little boy. But he don't need to be around a man like me who's drunk half the time and can't hold a job longer than six months . . . . Oh, jeez, why am I telling you this?" But tell he did.

Les went on to say he'd tried and tried to stop drinking, but he just couldn't seem to do it. He knew that booze had a power over him and it was destroying him. Maybe there was no hope for a guy like him.

As I watched in amazement, Dad put his arm around Les's shoulder. In a minute they were praying that he would be set free from alcoholism.

A short while later, another man came over. Jim just wanted to talk. In ten minutes, he was deep into telling Dad about all the trouble he was having in his marriage. His wife was threatening to leave him for another guy, and it was breaking his heart.

"I love her so much. But she says I don't care about her. What can I do? How can I get her to stay?"

I set about heating some beans over the fire. And Dad talked to Jim for quite awhile. Once again, the two of them wound up praying together.

This wasn't going the way I had pictured it. Weren't bikers supposed to be carefree? Happy go lucky?

I even felt some pains of jealousy when one young guy, who looked about my age, began talking to Dad about his relationship with his own father.

"I just can't talk to the man," he said.

"Oh, sure you can," Dad told him. He draped his arm around the kid's shoulder in fatherly fashion. "After all, he's your father. He loves you!"

Before that conversation was over, the young man was in tears. "When I get home, I'm going to go over to Dad's place and see if we can work things out. The truth is, I give him fits, and I know it. He really ain't so bad."

My chest was aching. It hurt to see my dad talking to this guy in such a helpful, fatherly way.

Suddenly, I realized that I wanted to be the one he talked to like that. The one whose shoulder he put his arm around. The one he *listened* to.

But at the moment, if he had tried to talk to me that way, I would have sneered at him. Deep down, it was what I really wanted. But what was holding me back?

Late into the first evening, Dad was busy giving pastoral counsel. He might as well have hung up a sign that said: *Caring Father—Line Forms Here.*

One guy had recently lost his job and was on the edge of despair.

A young woman was terribly depressed because men kept using her and dumping her. She'd been thinking about suicide.

Another woman confided, "I had an abortion two years ago. Now I can't have babies." Her grief was terrible.

It was one of the strangest things I've ever seen. How were these people being drawn to Dad. Did they see something in him I'd missed?

Dad was in his element. One by one, he told each person about the love of Christ. Almost without exception, they said they'd love to be prayed for.

Later that evening, Dad sought out one of the men who had been responsible for organizing the rally.

"I was just wondering," Dad asked him, "Is there any kind of a spiritual emphasis at these rallies?"

"Spiritual emphasis?" The man had a blank look in his eyes as he shook his head. "I'm not sure I know what you mean."

"You know . . . a chaplain."

The man's face brightened.

"Oh, well, sure. There's Chaplain Bob."

"Great! Where is he. I'd like to talk to him."

"We were directed to a small tent about fifty yards or so back in the woods.

A man was sitting in a folding chair in front of the tent.

"Excuse me," Dad asked. "Are you Chaplain Bob?"

"You bet your sweet a— I am."

With what seemed to be a tremendous effort, "Chaplain Bob" got up from his chair. Then he came reeling in our direction.

"Who the h— are you?" Chaplain Bob was drunk out of his mind.

We gave him our names. He stunk. "You fellas wouldn't have any wine, would you?"

This staggering, bleary-eyed, incoherent drunk was the "chaplain?" Obviously, the title was a big joke.

Late at night, I heard Dad tossing in his sleeping bag. Later, I would learn he'd stayed awake far into the night, praying about the day's events. There were so many questioning people here. People looking for answers to life's questions and hurts.

These men and women desperately needed to know how to find new life through faith in Jesus. There ought to be a ministry designed to reach out to people who rode motorcycles.

"Please God," he prayed, just before falling asleep, "send someone to help these people. But please . . . don't let it be me."

Someone. But who?

CHAPTER 5

Sharp Turns Ahead

For weeks after we returned home, Dad kept thinking about all the people he had met there in Texas. How confused and lonely they were. How much they needed Jesus. For the first time, he began to think that maybe God had more than a father-son reconciliation in mind when He gave him the idea to buy a motorcycle. He began to see that motorcycles and evangelism could go together in a very big way. But still . . . he didn't really want to be the one to put them together.

Over the next few weeks, he spent quite a bit of time talking to his friends about his Texas experiences.

He felt strongly that there should be an organized effort to take the gospel to people who rode motorcycles, but most of the people he talked to didn't think it was a very good idea.

"Motorcyclists? Are you kidding? Those people are beyond reach."

"Bikers? You mean those hairy guys with all the tatoos? Those people who don't do anything but drink, smoke and fight? No . . . I think you'd better forget about it."

There were a few who thought it was a pretty good idea, but they didn't want to be the ones to do it.

"If God's put it in your heart . . . then maybe you should move on ahead," one said.

"No . . ." he answered. "I really don't think I'm the one.

I think God just wants to use me to get somebody else to get it started."

Dad was really in a dilemma. He couldn't get those bikers out of his mind, but he couldn't seem to get anyone else to share his vision.

Over the next few weeks, he was still on the road a lot—as much as he had ever been, in fact. But when he was home, the two of us were often together on our motorcycles, exploring the highways and back roads of western Arkansas and eastern Oklahoma.

I'd like to tell you that getting a motorcycle and traveling with Dad made an immediate change in my behavior—but it didn't.

My ambition was still to be an outlaw biker. Now that I had a bike of my own, I figured I was half-way there.

I began hanging out with several other guys at school who also had motorcycles. We weren't all that bad, but sometimes we thought we were.

One time, eight of us were riding our motorcycles through the town of Mena, when some nerdy kid in a Pinto decided to flip us off. I don't know why he did it. It was a pretty stupid thing to do, seeing as how he was vastly outnumbered, and he didn't actually look like the type who could hold his own in a street fight anyway.

Naturally, we all took off in hot pursuit.

Left, right, right, left, right again—up and down the streets of Mena.

We stayed after him for at least forty-five minutes. There was no way in the world we were going to let him lose us. He would have been better off if he had just given up and let us catch him quickly, because after forty-five minutes of roaring up and down the streets of Mena, we had all worked ourselves into a pretty good lather. At first, we were just angry. Now, we were furious.

Finally, he took a wrong turn into a parking lot behind Mena High School. There was no way out. We had him.

He locked his doors and tried to roll up the windows, but he wasn't fast enough.

We pulled him out of his car and began taking turns pounding on him.

But before we could do any serious damage, we were interrupted by the loud roar of a four-barrel carburetor, followed quickly by the scream of a siren, and the squeal of brakes. Our high-speed chase through Mena had attracted the attention of the town police.

Two patrolmen jumped out of their car with guns drawn and loudly ordered us to stand still.

Our victim wisely told the police that he didn't want to press charges, so they had no choice but to let us go.

But not without a warning from one of the cops.

"From now on, we don't want to ever see more than two of you in town at the same time. Do you understand me?"

"Yes, sir."

"I mean it!" He pointed his finger at me. "If we ever see more than two of you together, we'll arrest you for disturbing the peace. And while you're sitting in jail, we'll think up some reason to keep you there."

Before they let us go, the cops checked all of our licenses and took down our names and phone numbers. As always, I made a big point of telling them that my dad was a preacher. By that time, Dad was pretty well known in the area, especially since he had a weekly broadcast on the local radio station.

"Maybe you've heard him on the radio?"

"So . . . you're Pastor Shreve's son?"

"That's right!"

"Does your dad approve of this?"

I started to shoot him a smart answer, but then thought

better of it. I wanted to be an outlaw, yes, but I didn't really want to go to jail. So I just stood there in silence.

"Your dad's a good man, son. Maybe you'd better start listening to what he says."

It wasn't until after the cops had left that we had all sorts of wise remarks to make. Basically, we just felt like the baddest guys around. We had finally arrived. Here in the Mena/Hatfield area we were outlaws—of a sort, anyway.

We rode together a lot after that, and on one occasion— Easter weekend, in fact—we all took a trip over to Oklahoma. There was a pretty little blue lake there, surrounded by woods of oak and elm, and there were some great roads for motorcycle riding. We planned to spend the entire weekend camping out and riding our bikes.

Early on Easter Sunday, I decided to go for an "Easter sunrise" bike ride. I think it was mostly because I was afraid my parents were going to come looking for me, to try to drag me to church.

I don't know what happened. Maybe I hit a pothole in the road. Maybe my chain broke. Maybe I fell asleep while riding, but one minute I was riding my bike along a peaceful, wooded road, and the next thing I knew I was flying through the air. I remember seeing my motorcycle in the air above me, and the ground rushing up to meet me, and then everything went black.

When I came to, I was lying in a culvert underneath a twisted and bent hunk of metal that had been my motorcycle. I was drenched with gasoline. I wiped my face and my hand came away covered with blood.

I pushed myself out from under my bike. As I struggled to my feet, an excruciating pain shot through my lower leg.

I could see a farmhouse a short distance away. I limped. I crawled. Several times I almost passed out from the pain.

Finally, though, I reached the house, limp-crawled up to the front porch and knocked weakly on the door.

A moment later, I was peering into the half made-up face of a woman wearing an obviously new and starchy Easter dress.

She took one look and started screaming.

Her husband, who was somewhere in the back of the house, apparently getting dressed for church, came running out in his underwear. His wife was still screaming, and he probably thought I was some sort of deranged attacker, leaning there against the house, bloody, ragged, and with long hair sticking out in every possible direction.

Pulling his wife out of the doorway, he prepared to punch me.

I held up my hands. "Please. I need help."

"Oh. What happened? Are you okay?"

"I had an accident," I moaned.

The man wasn't anxious to have me come inside and bleed all over his carpet. But he was nice enough to help me into his pickup and take me back to where my friends were camped. Along the way, he stopped and put my pathetic-looking motorcycle in the back of his truck.

My friends managed to get me to the sheriff's office in the nearest town. They asked him to take me to the hospital, but he didn't think that was necessary. Instead, he said I could lie down in one of the cells until my parents were able to come get me. By now I was sure my ankle was broken and asked if he could at least send for a doctor. "Oh, you'll probably feel better by morning," he said off-handedly.

I knew he didn't want to go out of his way to help me because I was a biker, and he didn't like bikers. He wasn't mean or anything. He just didn't figure I was worth a whole lot of extra effort. Once again, I had run into the attitude that people who ride motorcycles are somehow a little bit lower than "normal" human beings.

As it turned out, the jail was right next door to a church.

"Listen," I told the sheriff. "My dad is a preacher. Can you please ask someone at the church to try to get word to him? Tell him that I've been hurt. Maybe he can come and get me."

"Sure, I can do that."

He sent word to the pastor of the church, but no one responded.

Nobody came to see if I needed anything, or how badly I had been hurt. Nobody said, "Don't worry, we're trying to get hold of your parents."

From my cell, I could see dozens of people, all dressed in their Easter best, arriving for the service. Then I saw them leave after the service, heading home to Easter dinners and egg hunts with their children. But I never saw anybody so much as cast a glance in the jail's direction.

"Thanks a lot, people," I thought. "Thanks for caring."

Meanwhile, my friends had headed back to Arkansas to see if they could get help. It wasn't until late that afternoon that they came back with one of their fathers. He took me home, then went and found my parents at church and told them what had happened.

Mom came home immediately and took me to the nearest emergency room.

It turned out that my ankle was broken, as I had already known, and the rest of my injuries consisted of contusions and abrasions. Thankfully, there were no serious internal injuries.

Still, I was on crutches for weeks, and during that entire time I was constantly picking pieces of gravel out of my skin.

My bike's injuries were even worse than mine. It took

every penny of my savings to get it fixed. And even then, I wasn't sure I ever wanted to ride again. For weeks, I had terrible nightmares in which I relived the accident in great detail.

Sometimes I'd be sitting in class at school and I'd have a flashback. The pain seemed so real that I'd feel sick.

I didn't think I'd ever be able to get back on a motorcycle.

It was Dad who reminded me that riding a bike was just like riding a horse. If you were thrown, you had to get right back on.

"Look," he said, "you don't have to keep riding motorcycles, but you do have to ride one more time. If you ride it . . . and you don't like it . . . you can stop. But you owe it to yourself to give it a good try."

I knew he was right.

And so, on a Saturday afternoon, we wheeled my newly repaired bike out into the street. I cautiously climbed aboard, kicked it into life, and took off for a short spin around the block.

I was shaking as I wobbled off down the street. My knees were so weak, I was afraid I couldn't even hold the bike up.

But as I rounded the corner and headed down the next street, my confidence suddenly began to come back. It felt so good to have my motorcycle beneath me. It felt so natural.

By the time I got back home I had a big smile on my face.

"Looks like you're enjoying yourself," Dad said.

"Yeah . . . I guess I am."

"So, you feel okay?"

"Yeah . . . yeah, I do."

"Good. Because I've been thinking about something. How'd you like to take a little ride . . . to Seattle?"

"Seattle? That's clear across the country!"

"I know. I figure it would take us about four weeks."

"Four weeks?"

He went on to explain that his denominational convention was being held in Seattle that year, and he thought it offered a great opportunity for us to spend an extended amount of time together.

He already had the trip planned. We'd head up through Montana . . . take a short side trip into Canada . . . and maybe even drop down into Mexico on our way home. We'd be traveling over 6,000 miles. Along the way, we'd hit a number of camps and rallies, and get to know some of our fellow bikers.

"But . . . how will Mom feel about this?"

He smiled. "Your mother's in favor of anything that will help to bring us together. I think you know that."

I did. "Well . . . sure."

It turned out to be a fantastic adventure, even though we pushed ourselves hard, traveling hundreds of miles every day.

The trip across country strengthened Dad's resolve that *someone* ought to start an organization to minister to motorcyclists. Everywhere we went, he met people in trouble who desperately needed to know Jesus.

Almost every night after we made camp, he would find someone he could talk to about the Lord. As for me, while Dad was otherwise engaged, I'd go off and look for a secluded spot where I could smoke some grass.

One morning, Dad approached me with a worried look. "Have you been feeling okay, Son? You don't look good."

"Me? Oh, I'm fine."

I don't know if Dad knew what I had been up to, but at any rate, he didn't push it.

I was enough to actually hide some marijuana in the grillwork of my bike and drive across the border into Canada.

Thankfully, I didn't get caught. I'm sure God was looking out for Dad because I could have done some serious damage to his reputation—and I could have gotten myself into serious trouble with the authorities.

At the Seattle convention Dad tried, again, to talk to people about the importance of beginning a ministry to motorcyclists and bikers. Most of them listened politely, but without very much enthusiasm. Same old story. They just didn't see the need.

But Dad did. Although I didn't know it at the time—or maybe I knew it, but didn't really care—Dad had shed a lot of tears over me. He had spent countless hours in heart-felt prayer regarding the gulf that existed between us. He had agonized over the distance I had placed between myself and God.

And, as my father agonized over me, he sensed the pain in the Father-heart of God. The heavenly Father was also agonizing, weeping, calling out in love to His children who had turned their backs on Him. Dad understood, as he had never understood before, the pain and anguish God felt over even one soul that had wandered away. He was more and more convinced that God was calling him to take the message of his Father's love to those lost souls on the highways and byways of America.

On our way home, we traveled through Glacier National Park in Montana. It started raining just as we passed through the western boundary of the park. Then it turned to snow. By the time we got to the lodge at the center of the park, the gloves I was wearing were literally frozen to my bike. I tried to take my hands off the handlebars, and they wouldn't budge. I finally had to pull them out of the gloves, leaving the gloves themselves stuck to the motorcycle.

That was the first and only time during that entire four weeks that we spent the night inside. From there, we were planning on heading south, going all the way into Mexico. But that night, we called home to talk to Mom, and, as I talked to her I could hear the crickets chirping in the background. Suddenly, I was very homesick. We 'd had a terrific time, but I was ready to go home.

So was Dad. After all . . . he had some serious thinking and praying to do. And, if he was hearing God right, he had a whole lot of work ahead of him.

CHAPTER 6

When the Right Woman Comes Along

Meanwhile, I had my own dreams. I dreamed of being an outlaw biker. Or perhaps the lead guitarist for a loud rock band. Those were my twin ambitions. Someone every one else looked up to and respected—and maybe even feared a little bit.

I was attending school in Mena at the time, even though we lived in Hatfield . . . and, like most tough guys, I ditched school whenever I felt like it.

One day, as I was indulging in that favorite pastime, I happened to be walking past Hatfield High School. Three girls, sitting at their desks waiting for a math class to begin, looked out the window and saw me go by.

"There goes Herbie Shreve," one of them said. "I think he's cute."

"I don't like him," one of the other girls sniffed.

"You don't? Why not?"

"Because I think he's a jerk!"

"A jerk? How can you say that?"

"Easy. It's true."

The girl who had such a low opinion of me was Diane Callahan. And Diane didn't like me because I was the opposite of just about everything she stood for. Diane was a committed Christian. She had attended revivals where Dad preached. As far as she was concerned, he didn't deserve a rebellious son like me. Beyond that, Diane was an excellent student. I did just enough to get by, and sometimes not even that. She tried hard to be a model citizen, to be a good example for Christ. Me, on the other hand, the worse my reputation was, the better I felt about myself!

It was about this time that the teachers and principal in Mena decided they had had enough of my tough-guy act. They were tired of my cutting classes, and even more fed up with some of the other stupid things I did—like challenging teachers to "meet me after school" when I didn't like the way they were treating me in class.

Finally, it was suggested that I should transfer to Hatfield. Actually, it was more than a suggestion. It was an order.

One person who was not terribly happy to see me arrive at her school was Diane. Still, almost from the very first day I was there, she began seeking me out. It was like I was her very own personal reclamation project.

I immediately found out two important things about Diane: She was blunt. And she was persistent.

When she saw me doing something she didn't like, she let me know about it—face to face.

I particularly remember the first time she came and sat down next to me in the cafeteria. I was shocked that she even wanted to sit at my table and flabbergasted when she started in on me.

"I don't know who you think you're fooling, but I know you're not nearly as bad as you think you are."

I almost choked on my milk.

"What are you talking about?"

"You just don't want to be identified as a Christian—that's all. You're into all this rebellion stuff just because you want to make up for being a preacher's kid."

She looked so serious I had to laugh.

"You're crazy," I said, shaking my head at her nerve.

But deep down, I knew she wasn't crazy. She was the

43

only one who dared to speak the truth to me. And, to tell you the truth, if a guy had said the things that Diane said to me, I probably would have punched him.

But for some reason, I could accept it from her.

I knew right away that she was somebody special. She was pretty, yes. She was popular. She was very bright. And I was actually quite flattered that she thought I was worth saving.

But it was something beyond all those things that made her so special. There was just something about her. And for that reason, she also scared me just a little bit.

In a way, I wanted Diane to be able to turn *my* life around—to convince me that there really was a God in heaven who loved me and wanted to take charge of my life. But I wasn't sure if I could ever come to believe the way she did. One thing was sure. Such faith wouldn't come easy.

What I didn't understand was that Diane's persistence was a reflection of the Father-heart of God. In a way, it wasn't so much Diane Callahan who was trying to rescue me from the "junk heap" of life as it was God Himself who was relentless in His efforts to win me back to Him. Even if I pretended I wasn't listening to her, or tried to put her down for her faith, God's love would not let her give up on me.

I had given up on Him, but He wouldn't do that to me. I had told Him I had no use for Him. I had told Him to leave me alone. I had even told Him I didn't believe in Him. But He just kept answering back, "I love you." The only thing was, I didn't want to hear how much He loved me. I didn't want to hear it from Dad. Nor did I want to hear it from Diane Callahan.

Still, if I was being honest with myself, I had to admit that I did enjoy talking with Diane, debating with her, and occasionally trying to shock her with my rough edges. She continued to hang in there and, I think even in spite of herself, came to think of me as her friend.

It was about this time that I had my accident in Oklahoma and came back to school on crutches. Diane was one of the few who seemed genuinely sympathetic, and because of that I finally decided that I was going to do something I'd been thinking about for a long time . . . ask her out for an honest-to-goodness date.

When my friends heard I was going to ask her out, they made fun of me.

"What's the point?" one of them said, pointing to my crutches. "What can you do in *that* kind of shape?"

Boy . . . he didn't know Diane very well if he thought that any guy could *do* anything with her. She wasn't that kind of girl, and it kind of made me angry that he *thought* I could get anywhere with her.

Another friend thought I was crazy for even asking. He said a sweet Christian girl like Diane would never go out with the likes of me—and I was inclined to agree with him.

Still, there was going to be a Christian rock concert in the park Friday night. Maybe she'd think it was okay to let me take her to that. I couldn't ride a motorcycle in my condition, but I could drive, at least that far.

If she ever thought of me as a real tough guy, I'm sure that image was shattered the night I called and asked her for that date. It was one of the hardest things I had ever down. I almost hung up when she answered the phone, and then was angry at myself because I could hear my voice shaking when I asked if she'd go out with me. Mr. Tough Guy. Yeah . . . that was me.

"Listen," I said, "there's this Jesus freak thing in the park this weekend. And . . . I was just wondering . . . you wanna go with me?"

She didn't hesitate for a moment.

"Sure, that would be great!"

"Really?"

"Sure, I'd love to. What time do you want to pick me up?"

"Uh . . . well . . . don't you think you'd better ask your parents?"

"It'll be fine with them."

She seemed so sure.

"Okay then . . . great!" I was trying not to sound too excited. "I'll pick you up around 6:30?"

"Sounds great."

As it turned out, Diane told her parents she had a date with Herbie Shreve, "the preacher's son." What's more, they knew that Diane had been praying since she was a little girl that God would allow her to marry a preacher when she grew up.

We were only in high school, but you never know. I just might turn out to be the one their little girl had been praying for all those years.

For that reason, when I got to Diane's house to pick her up on Friday night, her folks were both there waiting to meet me.

And you should have seen her father's jaw drop when I walked in the door. He didn't say a word. He just stood there, seemingly in shock, looking suspiciously at my hair, which tumbled down around my shoulders. I'm sure he was thinking that they'd have to look a little bit further for that preacher.

As for me, I wasn't really sure how to treat a "nice" girl. Was I supposed to open the door for her? What was I supposed to say to her? It was strange, because I talked to her almost every day in school, but this was different.

Despite that rather rough beginning, I wound up having one of the best times of my life. And that, despite the fact that I had neither touched nor kissed her, and I had spent the evening listening to Christian music.

That was a really weird weekend, because for the first time ever, I was actually anxious for Monday to come around. I just couldn't wait to see that girl again. Still, I didn't want to be too easy. I wouldn't admit to her that I liked her, that I thought she was special, or anything of the sort. I wanted to. But such tenderness didn't exactly fit the macho biker style I wanted to project.

As soon as I got my bike fixed and got off my crutches, I decided it was time to put this relationship to the acid test. It was time to see how Diane handled herself on a motorcycle.

I rode out to her house and found her sweeping off the front porch.

"I came to see if you wanted to go for a ride."

She wasn't too sure.

"I'll have to ask my dad."

"I'd rather you didn't," I said. "That might mean the end of a good thing."

"Well . . . he's not here right now."

"Where is he?"

"He went up to the chicken house."

I knew that there was very little chance the man would say yes to his daughter taking a quick spin on the back of my bike. I had to move fast.

"Look," I said, "we won't go very far. We'll probably be back before he gets home. He doesn't even have to know."

I didn't expect her to say, "Okay," but she did, and quickly hopped off the porch and onto the back of my bike.

With Diane clinging to me, I took off in the direction of Talimena Drive—a twisting, turning mountain road which, because of its curves, is regarded as one of the ten best motorcycle roads in the United States. I knew that road well. In fact, my friends and I used to dare each other to ride it at night with our lights off.

Before we started up the mountain, I pulled off to the side of the road, turned off my motor, and told her a little bit about what to expect. "Now the way you ride a motorcycle is that you just don't fight it. If I lean, you lean. You try to be one with me."

She said she understood.

I figured that understanding would go flying off into space as soon as we hit the first major curve.

Well, when we hit that curve, I had to look back and make sure the girl was still with me. I'd taken a lot of girls on that ride, and they almost always instinctively leaned the wrong way, which made it very hard to control the motorcycle. But Diane was doing exactly what she was supposed to do. We were leaning over so far on some of those curves that my pipes were scraping the pavement, and she was as calm and cool as if she'd been riding a bike for years.

When we got to the top of the road, we took off our helmets and the first words out of her mouth were, "Oooh, I like that!"

My response was, "Ooooh, I like you!"

This was indeed a special relationship! Any girl who felt that way about motorcycles had a very big piece of my heart.

Over the next few weeks, I began seeing more of Diane, a fact which most of my teachers noticed with varying degrees of disapproval.

One of them went so far as to tell me that if I wanted to pass his class, I'd better stop dating her.

I walked out of his classroom with a bit of a swagger. I wasn't upset. I was highly complimented that he thought that much of me.

Thankfully, after awhile, when that teacher saw that I

really cared for Diane, his attitude softened. And I did manage to pass his class—just barely!

A couple of other teachers weren't quite so blunt, but they let it be known that they thought a lot of Diane and that I'd better not do anything to hurt her. Of course not. I already knew this little girl was the best thing I'd ever found. I wouldn't have hurt her for the world.

I was on my "best" behavior when I was with Diane. Oh, I smoked, and I swore, but I never drank or did drugs when she was with me.

But then again, a lot of times, I'd take her home at the end of the evening, and then go out with my friends and do both of those things. The truth was that I was doing quite a bit of dope in those days, but I didn't tell Diane about it because I knew she wouldn't like it.

I was also doing a little bit of drug dealing during that time. Nothing major, but I occasionally sold some pot or pills to some of the guys I hung around with.

One night, as Diane and I drove through Mena on our way to a movie, I looked in the rear-view mirror and saw one of my buddies in a car right behind us. I had promised to sell the guy some drugs, and had them stashed in the trunk.

As soon as I could, I pulled into the courthouse parking lot and stopped.

"What's going on?" Diane wanted to know.

"Oh . . . uh . . . it's a friend of mine." I was fishing for something to say. "I . . . uh . . . borrowed some eight-track tapes from him, and he probably just wants them back. I'll be right back."

I hopped out of the car, ran back to get the drugs out of the trunk, made the deal, and then hurried back to Diane. She seemed fine. She wasn't at all suspicious.

But as we drove off, a terrible thought hit me. What if the

police had come along? If they had busted me, she'd be in trouble, too, because she was with me.

That would have been like taking a garment of the finest silk and trampling it into the mud. I made up my mind right then that I would never deal drugs again . . . and I never did. I didn't stop using them right away. I wasn't that strong. But Diane's presence was starting to have a positive impact on my life.

I already knew that she was the kind of woman I wanted for my wife. The only problem was that I figured she was too smart to put up with me the way I was, so I slowly began putting my drugs away, trying to get myself into the sort of shape where she might at least consider me.

Not too long after that, I invited her over to meet Mom. She came over after church on a Sunday, put on a pair of old blue jeans, and we spent the day "playing" and acting silly. We had a great time.

That night, Dad called from wherever he was on the road to get the latest news.

"Anything interesting happen today?" he asked.

"Well, yes, as a matter of fact it did," Mom replied. "I met Herbie's wife today."

"You met *who*? What are you talking about?"

"I met a really special girl today. And if Herbie doesn't mess it up, I think she'll be his wife some day."

Dad must have rolled his eyes when he heard that. I was only 16, and I wasn't showing the slightest inclination of being the marrying kind.

But what Dad didn't know was that Diane had stopped praying that God would give her a preacher.

"Lord, I know I've been asking you for years to allow me to marry a preacher. But I've changed my mind. I don't want a preacher now. I just want Herbie!"

A few days later, when Dad got home, he told me that he was anxious to meet this girl he had heard so much about. We arranged for her to come over for a cook-out on a Thursday evening, and I went to her house and picked her up on my motorcycle.

When we got back to my house, the air was thick with barbecue smoke, and Mom and Dad were both out in the yard, tending to hamburgers on the grill.

I hopped off the motorcycle and extended my hand to help Diane off. As she removed her helmet, I started to introduce her. "Dad, this is Diane."

"Hello, Diane, I'm pleased to . . . ." As her hair fell down around her shoulders, he saw her face for the first time and stopped in mid-sentence. For a moment, he looked like he didn't even know where he was, and I was sure he was going to drop the spatula he was holding.

But he quickly caught himself, and went on as if nothing had happened. ". . . meet you. I've been hearing a lot of good things about you."

I looked at Diane to see if she had noticed his strange behavior. If she had, she didn't let on, and the rest of the evening passed without further "weirdness" on his part.

Later on, I asked Dad what had happened, but he just shrugged it off. It wasn't until months later that he told me what had really happened.

Several years before this, he had preached one Sunday in a small country church, a few miles down the road from Hatfield.

Just before it was time for him to give his sermon, a young girl had come forward to play the piano and sing. My father had been touched by the girl's sweet spirit. So much so, in fact, that he had breathed a silent prayer, "Lord, I want that girl for Herbie."

I was just a boy at the time—no more than twelve or

thirteen years old—but my father just knew, somehow, that this little girl would be a perfect wife for me—someday.

He hadn't seen that girl again after that night, and had eventually forgotten all about her and his prayer for her.

Until, that is, Diane took off her helmet, and my father found himself looking into the face of the same sweet girl he had prayed for all those years ago.

At that moment, Dad knew, beyond any doubt, that Mom had been telling him the truth when she said, "I met Herbie's wife today."

What's more, Mom told me that she, too, had been praying for Diane, even though she had never met her. Because she had been very worried about my increasingly rebellious lifestyle, she had been praying that God would help me someday by bringing a good, Christian girl into my life to be my wife.

She told me, "That day you brought Diane over for the first time, I knew right away that she seemed familiar, but I couldn't remember where I'd met her.

"I thought about it all day, and every time I saw her I'd think, 'Where do I know that girl from?'

"And then it came to me. This is the girl I had been praying for. That's why she was so familiar."

Mom wasn't quite ready for God to bring that girl into my life just yet—seeing that I was only sixteen years old. But as far as she was concerned, there was no mistaking the fact that Diane was the one she'd been praying for.

Talk about being made for each other!

Diane was a wonderful influence. Just being around her began to soften my heart. What's more, her attitude toward Dad helped me to see things from a different perspective. For the first time in a long, long while, I began to feel a sense of pride in being Herb Shreve's son.

There were still problems between us, to be sure. I wasn't

ready to tell him I loved him. I had too much resentment in me for that. But I was civil to him—and even that was a step in the right direction.

Diane and I both graduated from high school in 1975—Diane graduated a year early, at seventeen—and we were married in July, with Dad performing the ceremony.

I still wasn't living for God in those days. Far from it. But in the midst of my rebellion, He reached down and gave me the greatest miracle of them all. My lover. My friend. My companion. My wife, Diane.

For the first time in a long, long while I felt content. Almost happy.

As far as I was concerned, if believing in God made Diane feel good, that was fine with me. But as for me, well . . . who needed Him?

I was about to find out.

CHAPTER 7

Put in Me a New Heart

After Diane and I were married, I took a job in the local sawmill.

I found out real quick about life in the "real world." It was tough as nails, and it didn't pay very well.

I worked with a bunch of guys who'd spent their lives at the sawmill. Some of them had been there for 20 or 25 years or more, and most of them were missing at least one or two fingers—and some more. These were good guys, tough guys, and I respected them. But I had nightmares in which I saw myself at 35 or 40, bent over from years of that hard work, and missing several fingers on each hand. That wasn't the way I wanted to spend my life.

It all came to a head for me one day when there was an article in the local newspaper saying that the federal government was going to raise the minimum wage. The guys I worked with were obviously very excited by that news.

"Wait a minute," I said. "You mean you guys are making minimum wage."

" 'Course," shrugged one grizzled old vet, pushing his cap back on his head with a hand that was missing half an index finger. "Everyone here makes minimum wage."

I thought he was pulling my leg.

"Look, I understand why I make minimum wage. I've only been here a few weeks. I just got out of high school.

But some of you guys have been here for years! You *must* make more than I do."

Some of the men laughed at my naivete.

" 'Fraid not," one of them said. "You're making minimum wage now . . . and if you're here in 30 years, you'll still be making minimum wage then."

I stewed about that all day. I wasn't going to spend the rest of my life slaving away for pennies.

I'd never thought much about college before. But all of a sudden, it sounded pretty good. I was smart enough. If I applied myself, I could make it in college. The more I thought about it, the more I knew that was what I was going to do.

Finally, I went and found the foreman, and told him I needed to talk to him.

"Yeah? What do you want?"

"I've just decided that I don't want to spend the rest of my life working here. So I'd appreciate it if you'd consider this my two-week's notice."

He looked totally bored and disinterested.

"If that's how you feel, forget the two weeks. Just leave now."

"Well, I . . ." I wasn't ready to be without an income just yet.

"Go on! Get out of here. You're through."

"H—, yes, I'm through," and I stomped off, thinking that the guy was lucky I didn't pop him one.

Diane and I immediately began making plans to head off to college, and because we were married and had virtually no income, we were able to get significant financial aid. I can see clearly, looking back on it now, how God was directing my steps. Even in my state of rebellion against Him, He was looking out for me—guiding me, protecting me. I know, now, that Dad never stopped praying for me, and God was honoring his prayers. Thank God for a father's love!

Meanwhile, Dad continued to spend much of his time thinking about how good it would be if *somebody* would start a ministry aimed specifically at people who rode motorcycles. But at the same time, the more he thought about it and prayed it, the more he was convinced that he didn't want to be the one to do it.

Part of the reason for this was that he loved to put on a suit and tie and preach from the pulpit. What's more, he was really good at it. Even when I wasn't living for God, I had to admit that something happened when my dad preached. He spoke with power, and people were visibly moved. He always got a great response.

He liked seeing that happen. And he didn't want to give it up to go riding around the country on a motorcycle, wearing jeans and leathers.

But then something happened. He started feeling really sick.

He had chest pains. He couldn't seem to catch his breath. And even though he was worn out from dealing with whatever was going on in his body, he couldn't sleep. Night after night, he'd fall into bed exhausted, only to find his sleepiness slowly beginning to fade away.

Doctors couldn't figure out what was wrong. They thought maybe it was related to his diet, or that it had something to do with spending so much time on the road.

Whatever it was, they didn't know how to help him, and so he just had to contend with the insomnia. It was a rare night when he wouldn't slip out of bed, go into the living room, and spend hours reading the Bible. One night, as he was doing that, a particular verse of scripture seemed to almost leap off the page:

"I have set before thee an open door that no man can

shut." As he read those words, his heart began beating rapidly. He sensed that God was speaking directly to him.

The verse went on to say that there would be opposition as he tried to go through this new door, but that God would be with him and help him.

He read it again, "I have set before thee an open door that no man can shut."

What did this mean? Was God calling him into a motorcycle ministry after all?

"Lord," he prayed, "you know I'll go wherever You want me to go, and do whatever you want me to do. I just hope you don't want me to start riding a motorcycle on a full-time basis. But if that *is* what You have in mind . . . please give me a willing and obedient heart."

It was the very next day, or perhaps the day after that, that Dad got a telephone call from a Baptist church in Greenwood, Arkansas. Seems they were looking for a new pastor, and they wanted him to come down and candidate for the position. That meant that he'd meet with the selection committee, preach for them on Sunday morning, and if they liked what they heard, they'd be moving to Greenwood.

Everything went great in Greenwood, and Mom and Dad came back to Hatfield knowing the job was theirs if they wanted it.

And, certainly, they wanted it!

After all, the Lord had given them that scripture about an "open door." Surely, this was what He had been talking about.

Dad began to think that this whole matter was the reason he hadn't been able to sleep. The illness and the sleeplessness had all been part of God's attempt to get his attention.

All of the pieces were beginning to come together. And

he was so thankful that the Lord was not calling him into full-time motorcycle ministry.

A few days later, the official phone call came asking him to take over the pulpit of Greenwood Baptist Church. He said yes, and he and Mom made plans to take a second trip to Greenwood, this time to pick out a house.

But that night, Dad still couldn't sleep. He thought now that everything was resolved, he'd sleep like a baby. Instead, it was another long night of tossing and turning.

Finally he gave up, got out of bed and went into the living room to read the Bible.

He opened it at random, and it fell open to the very same scripture: "I have set before thee an open door . . . ."

Why was that scripture coming back again?

"I've misunderstood God," he thought. "If this was the door He wanted me to go through, then He wouldn't be coming back to me on this."

First thing the next morning, he told my mother what had happened. She agreed that God must not want them to go to Greenwood. And so, even though it was a very tough thing to do, Dad called and told the people in Greenwood he would not be able to take the job they had offered.

Dad was convinced he had done the right thing, but that didn't seem to improve the situation either. Over the next few days his condition took a drastic turn for the worse. He was so sick that Mom thought he was going to die. He couldn't even get out of bed without assistance.

Then one weekend when Diane and I came for a visit, I was frightened to see how pale and small he looked. Herb Shreve was a big man, and it looked like he was almost shrinking into the bed.

"Dad," I said, "You have *got* to go to the doctor."

"Well . . . I . . . ."

"I'm going to take you to the doctor if I have to *carry* you!"

He just looked at me, too weak to argue.

"In fact, I'm going to make an appointment right now!"

He nodded.

I went into the kitchen, called our family doctor, and told him that my dad needed to come in immediately. He said he'd work us in. Together, Mom and I helped Dad get dressed, walked him to the car, and then drove him down to the doctor's office. I drove, with Dad sitting in the front passenger seat, and my mother rode in the back with Kelly.

Seeing Dad outside in the light of day increased my concern. He just didn't look right. His skin was grey, his eyes seemed to be sunken into his head, and the short walk to the car left him gasping for breath.

The doctor took one look at him and said, "I'm going to call the hospital right now, and tell them you're coming."

He wouldn't really tell us what he was suspecting, only that we needed to get to the hospital *now*.

At the hospital, we were met by a grim-faced surgeon.

"Mrs. Shreve . . . your husband is a very sick man. It looks like it's his heart . . . ."

"Heart? How could he . . . ." Mom's hands were gripping the handle of her purse so tightly that her knuckles were turning white.

"There's some kind of blockage," the doctor explained. "He's going to need surgery . . . and pretty quick. How long has he been like this?"

The doctor said we had come just in time. A few more days might have been too late.

He went on to say that there was another problem, and that was that the kind of surgery and treatment he needed wasn't available locally. They were going to send him, by ambulance, to Fort Smith. Mom could ride along with him, if she wanted to, or we could come later, which ever worked best.

The surgery itself would be scheduled as quickly as possible. Perhaps even for the following day. It couldn't wait.

We weren't prepared for this. We knew he was sick, but we figured maybe they'd give him a shot, or some pills, and that would be the end of it. Dad was still a young man, in his early 40s. He'd always been strong. How in the world could he have a heart problem?

I know it's a cliché to say that you don't know what you have until you're faced with the prospect of losing it. But that's the way it was for me, sitting there in that hospital waiting room. I was overcome with remorse for the way I had felt toward my father for so many years. I didn't want to lose him. And, even though I didn't really believe in God, I offered up a silent prayer that he would make it through surgery. I even made a vow, to whom I don't know, that if Dad pulled through, from now on, I would make more of an effort to get along with him. Maybe that doesn't sound like much. But for me it was a very big step.

Dad's open-heart surgery was scheduled for first thing the following morning—and he almost didn't live through it.

That was one of the longest days of my life—waiting for the surgeon to come in and tell us that Dad was out of danger, that he was going to be okay.

But there were complications. An important piece of equipment malfunctioned. Because of that, Dad almost drowned in his own blood. At one point, we were informed that his chances of survival were less than 50/50. I'd be lying if I told you we weren't scared. We were. But Mom knew that odds like that don't mean anything when God is involved. There had been a time when her doctors had given her a zero chance of survival, and she had beat those odds. She knew that with God's help, Dad would pull through this.

Afternoon had turned into evening before the surgeon came back to us with some good news. Dad's condition had stabilized. His vital signs seemed to be good, and he was resting comfortably in the intensive care unit—at least as comfortably, as someone who's just had heart surgery can rest.

He spent most of the next month in the hospital, and when he came home, he had a surprise for Mom.

Sitting at the breakfast table with her one morning, he told her that he wanted to resign from the little church near Hatfield where he was now serving as pastor.

"But then what . . . ?"

"Shirley, something happened to me when I was in that hospital."

She got up to pour herself another cup of coffee.

"Uh huh?"

"God did something in me. I know what He wants me to do now. What's more, *I* want to do it, too."

"And it has to do with motorcycles?" She knew he had been struggling with this issue for some time.

He reached over and took her hand.

"You know how I've felt," he said. "I've wanted someone to start a ministry to people who ride bikes. I just didn't want it to be me.

"Well, when I was lying in that hospital bed, it's like God changed things. For the first time ever, I really have a strong desire to get out on the road and start telling these people about Jesus."

Mom nodded and smiled.

"In fact, it got to the point where it was almost all I could think about while I was lying there. I couldn't wait to get well, so I could get out on the road and start telling them about Jesus."

It seemed he had undergone more than one kind of heart surgery while in that Fort Smith hospital.

"You know, when you preach in a church, you're almost always talking to people who already know the Lord. But out there . . . . so many of these people are completely lost. They don't even know that God loves them. If only they knew about Jesus . . . ." Dad's voice trailed off and Mom thought for a moment that he was going to cry.

After a moment of silence, she said, "So what do you want to do?"

"Like I said, I want to resign from the church. And then, as soon as I'm able, I'll go out on my bike . . . hit a few rallies . . . and let the Lord take it from there."

She was ready to do whatever God wanted, but she was also practical.

"Have you thought about how we're going to survive while you're out there on the road? I mean . . . where will we live?"

"If this is the Lord's will . . . and I'm sure it is . . . He will provide."

As far as she was concerned, probably the biggest problem with Dad resigning his pastorate was that they lived in a house the church provided.

It wasn't the best or biggest house in town, but it was nice enough, and they didn't have to pay rent. If Dad gave up the church, they'd also have to give up the house.

My dad had an answer for that. Mom's folks owned an old house just outside of Hatfield. It hadn't been lived in in recent years, and it needed quite a bit in the way of repair.

Dad insisted that with a little bit of work, the place would do just fine. Mom wasn't keen on the idea, but if it was what God wanted, she was willing to go along with it.

"Are you sure this is what God wants you to do?" she asked.

"Yes."

She thought for a moment, and then said, "I'll make you a deal."

"What kind of deal?"

"You know that I want whatever God wants. And so I'm willing to give this a try . . . for thirty days."

Dad nodded, "Okay."

"But if, after thirty days, it really isn't working out, I want you to promise me that you'll give up the idea, come back home, and get a real job."

He laughed at her use of the words "real job."

"You've got yourself a deal."

Dad planned to hit a number of motorcycle rallies in Arkansas, Oklahoma and Texas. The first rally he attended was in Kerrville, Texas. It was a small event—no more than 100 or so people for a weekend get together. At Dad's first Sunday morning service, a dozen or so people showed up to hear him preach, and three of them gave their lives to Christ.

Every few nights, he would call home to let Mom know what was happening on the road. With every call, his excitement seemed to be growing. Everywhere he went, people were being saved. They were being set free from drugs and booze. He told us about tough, outlaw-type bikers who wept when they heard how much Jesus loved them.

Meanwhile, back at home, Mom was pretty excited, too. Somehow, God seemed to be stretching what little money she had. She didn't know how it was possible to get by for a month on so little money . . . but it was happening.

The same thing was happening out there on the road. Dad never had much money in his wallet, but he had enough to get by. Every time he was down to his last couple of dollars, someone would come up and give him a few dollars, saying that they wanted to support what he was doing.

By the time he got home, he and Mom both knew that the new motorcycle ministry was definitely operating under God's blessing.

On one of his first trips after that, Dad stopped into a shop to get some minor maintenance done on his bike and saw a motorcycle magazine lying on a counter. Up until that moment, he didn't even know such magazines existed. He picked it up and flipped through it, and as he did, he was impressed by the number and variety of ads, articles and, especially, letters to the editor.

It was obvious that there were a lot of people "out there," reading magazines like this one. Perhaps there were at least a few who shared his commitment to the Lord. He scribbled down the magazine's address, and a few days later, wrote and placed a small classified ad. The ad asked anyone who was interested in joining in a Christian Motorcyclists Association to write him, and it gave our home address in Hatfield.

It was several months before the ad ran in the magazine, and by that time, he had pretty much forgotten all about it.

When the magazine finally came out, he and Mom were in Florida. I was staying in the house, taking care of things. About the second or third day of their trip, I went to the post office and found our box full of cards and letters, all addressed to something called CMA.

I couldn't figure out what in the world CMA was, and I certainly didn't know why all this mail was coming to *our house.*

That night, when Mom called to see how things were going, I told her, "Fine . . . except that we got a whole bunch of mail today that doesn't belong to us."

"Really? What kind of mail?"

"Oh . . . cards . . . letters . . . all kinds of stuff . . . and all of it addressed to CMA."

"CMA?"

She sounded every bit as puzzled as I was.

"What's that mean?"

"I have no idea."

"Well, let me ask your father."

I listened as they discussed the matter, and then she came back on the phone.

"He doesn't know what it's all about either."

"Well, what am I supposed to do with it?"

"I don't know. I guess just mark it 'return to sender.' "

"All right. Well, you guys have a good time."

"We are."

As soon as I got off the phone, I got out a big black marker, and did just as she had suggested. I wrote "return to sender" on every one of those letters. And then, because I didn't like that big stack of mail sitting around the house, I took the whole lot down to the post office.

By the time I got back home, the phone was already ringing.

I ran to catch it and was surprised to hear Dad's voice.

"Herbie. Did you say that all those letters were marked 'CMA'?"

"Yeah . . . that's right."

"That's gotta mean Christian Motorcyclists Association."

"Christian what?"

"I put an ad in a magazine," he explained. "Don't send those letters back. Just hold on to them until we get home."

"Well . . . it's a little late for that." I told him what I had done. (So now you know what happened if you wrote a letter to CMA years ago, and got it back marked "return to sender.")

"Okay. That's all right. But if we get any more letters tomorrow, hang on to them."

"I will."

Sure enough, the next day we got about twice as many letters as the day before. And they continued to come for about a week. They came from men and women all over the United States, many of whom said they were thrilled by the prospect of getting involved in an organization that combined Christianity with motorcycling.

Some said they didn't have any idea there were any other Christian motorcyclists "out there." Some said it was like finding out they had a family they had never known about.

The response was beyond anything Dad had anticipated . . . and he wasn't sure what to do about it.

He called a businessman friend, H.E. Copeland, to ask for advice.

Copeland was a very strong Christian who also happened to be a successful businessman *and* a motorcyclist. He had been a source of encouragement from the time Dad had started talking about starting a group for Christian motorcyclists.

Of course, he was delighted to hear about the response to the ad, and he felt that papers should be drawn up, establishing the Christian Motorcyclists Association as a not-for-profit corporation.

There was only one problem with that. It was going to cost $100, and my dad didn't have $100 to spare.

No problem. Copeland did.

And so, the very next day, the Christian Motorcyclists Association officially came into existence!

CHAPTER 8

Kicking Into High Gear

Over the next few months, the Christian Motorcyclists Association grew like crazy, sometimes even against Dad's wishes.

A group of motorcyclists from Arizona wrote and said they wanted to form a local chapter of CMA. He wrote back and urged them not to do it, explaining that it had never been his intention to have an association consisting of local chapters.

Return mail informed him, politely, that they had *already* formed such a chapter, and they all thought it was a terrific idea. Soon thereafter, word came from other parts of the country, from people saying they, too, had formed chapters, and wanted more information about the national organization.

People were writing from all over the country, saying they wanted to join CMA. At that point, Dad wasn't really sure what form or shape CMA was going to take. He just knew that God's love was compelling him, and he was willing to be used in whatever way God saw fit.

Men like H.E. Copeland were willing to give sacrificially to get the organization off the ground. Copeland himself put up the money to purchase three acres of land along the highway between Mena and Hatfield.

A small, trailer type of office building had been erected on that land. Even though it was not much to look at, it was officially named and consecrated to the Lord as the new organization's headquarters.

It had electricity, but nothing else. No running water. No plumbing of any sort, in fact. But it was something tangible that gave a concrete reality to the CMA. A sign was even erected proclaiming this as the national headquarters of the Christian Motorcyclists Association.

For the first year-plus of the organization's existence, Mom kept all the records in a shoe box on a shelf in a closet. She wrote a personal letter to everyone who wrote in, and that was no easy task, because that involved writing *hundreds* of people.

During those early years of the organization, she was the glue that held things together. Not only did she keep track of all the records—financial and otherwise—but she kept everyone informed as to what was going on at "headquarters." And quite a few things were happening.

For example, one morning Dad received a phone call from a man who introduced himself as "Del Friend." He lived in Paris, Texas, which is a little over 100 miles from Hatfield.

"I've just joined this CMA, and I'd like to know a little more about it. Can I come over and talk to you?"

"Sure. When do you want to come?"

"How about right now? My wife and I can be there in a couple of hours."

"Come on," Dad replied. "I'll be here."

Dad gave him directions to the house and, true to his word, Del and his wife pulled up exactly two hours later.

Del knew immediately that my folks were definitely *not* in this for the money. They had spent quite a bit of time fixing up the old house by now, but it was still a far cry from anything that was going to show up in a magazine like "Better Homes and Gardens," or "House Beautiful."

Del and his wife came in and sat down and Dad started to explain his reasons for starting CMA.

During the middle of his explanation, Del suddenly interrupted him.

"You mean this is an honest-to-God ministry?"

Dad was taken back a bit by that question.

"Of course, it's a ministry. I wouldn't be doing it otherwise."

A big smile spread across Del Friend's face.

"That's great! Just great! I was afraid this might be just something for fun—you know, a ride-and-eat type of thing."

Dad shook his head. "I just want to bring people to Jesus."

"That's exactly what I wanted to hear."

He wanted to know if CMA had an office, so Dad took him down and gave him a tour of the organization's "national headquarters."

They walked around the property while Dad shared more of his vision for CMA. Part of that vision, in those early days, consisted of improvements to the headquarters. It needed a well for water, and a septic tank. Dad also envisioned a pavilion where worship services and rallies could be held.

Friend was so impressed that he decided he wanted to pay for the installation of the well and the septic tank.

The next day found him and Dad back out at the property, measuring for the improvements. Because Dad was still recuperating from open heart surgery, he had to take a break and sit down every once in awhile. And so, while his newfound friend was pacing off the area, he went over and sat down on an old overturned can that was sitting on the ground nearby.

Tape-measure in hand, Friend was pacing off the area.

"Okay, the septic tank should go . . . right about here. And then, the well has to be at least 15 feet away."

He began walking in Dad's direction.

"Let's see . . . nine feet . . . ten feet . . . ."

Fifteen feet came exactly to where my dad was sitting on the old overturned can.

Dad got up and picked up the can. Underneath was a perfectly drilled well that neither had known was there. Both men just looked at each other in amazement. All this time, that can had been sitting on top of a well drilled by the previous property owner! Much of the work had been done before they even arrived at the property that morning!

Because of that head start, before that day was over, the land was equipped with a septic tank, a well, and a water pump.

That's the way things went in the early days of CMA. Miracles—both great and small—were a daily occurrence as God built His organization from the ground up.

It wasn't too long after this, while Diane and I were at college, that my parents' house burned down. But as it turned out, even that had all the marks of a miracle.

It happened during the summer of 1977.

Up until then, Mom and Kelly had gone on the road only occasionally. Dad had usually gone by himself. But as he was getting ready to head out on a long trip, he suddenly felt compelled to take them with him. He didn't know why. He just knew that he couldn't leave them home. They *had* to go.

Mom didn't like the idea. For one thing, she had promised one of the local churches that she would run their Vacation Bible School that summer. For another, my dad had one motorcycle, no sidecar, and she didn't know how he expected them all to go.

And then, too, nobody was drawing an official salary

from CMA in those days, and she didn't know how they could afford for the whole family to spend a month or more on the road.

But Dad wouldn't hear any of her objections.

"I can't get it out of my mind," he told her. "I just know that you're supposed to go with me."

"Well then, what are you going to do?"

"I guess I'll have to find a sidecar, and then I'll see if I can borrow the money to pay for it."

Mom just smiled. She knew chances were very slim that any bank would loan my dad several thousand dollars for a sidecar for his motorcycle. She figured that if he got turned down once or twice, maybe he'd forget this idea of her and Kelly going with him.

Over the next few weeks, Dad looked diligently for a sidecar, but there wasn't one to be had. He simply could not find one anywhere—at least not a used one that he might be halfway able to afford.

But just when he was about to give up, he got a phone call from his old friend H.E. Copeland.

"Hey, Herb," Copeland said, "I've got a motorcycle-sidecar rig here I'm fixing to sell. You wouldn't know anyone who wants to buy one, would you?"

"That depends. How much are you asking?"

"Well," Copeland laughed, "that depends, too. For you? Or for someone else?"

Copeland's rig was a beauty—a brand new Harley, beautifully dressed, with only about 5,000 miles on it. It had to be worth at least $8,000.

"For me."

"Well, if you want it, my price is $3500."

Dad didn't bat an eyelash. "You've just made yourself a deal," he said.

Once he got off the phone, Dad went off by himself and

began to pray. He didn't know what to do, because he didn't have $3,500. He was lucky if he had three dollars and fifty cents. But this was such an excellent deal, and he felt certain the Lord wanted him to take Mom and Kelly on this trip. He also felt, somehow, that if he left them home, something terrible might happen to them.

As he prayed, he felt convinced that God was telling him to go ahead and write a check for the sidecar. "I will supply the money you need," God seemed to be saying.

Now, as far as I know, there have only been one or two times in Dad's life when he's taken such a big risk. He is not the kind of man to say "God told me," because he wants to do something, and he has always taught that God is not compelled to cover anyone's mistakes.

Writing a check without money in the bank to cover it, was totally foreign to my father's way of doing things. But this was one occasion when Dad felt sure God was saying, "Go ahead."

Because there was a small mechanical problem, the sidecar wasn't ready until the very day Dad was supposed to leave on the trip. The plan was that Kelly, who was now six, would travel with him from the start, but Mom would stay home to take care of a few things. Then, she would take the bus to Kansas to meet up with the two of them at one of their scheduled stops there.

So far, no money had fallen out of the blue. But Dad had the assurance that God was in this, so he went over to his friend's house, picked up the sidecar rig, and wrote out a check for $3500.

Then he went home, packed his things, loaded Kelly into the sidecar, kissed my mother goodbye, and headed out of town. On his way, he stopped by the local bank.

Wearing his leathers and boots, and leading Kelly by the hand, he went inside and asked to speak to the loan officer.

"And what do you need, Pastor Shreve?"

"I need to borrow $3500 to buy a motorcycle sidecar rig."

"What kind of sidecar do you have in mind?"

"Well . . . it's outside if you'd like to see it."

"Oh, I don't suppose that will be necessary, Reverend."

Now you know as well as I do, that banks don't normally do business that way. Especially not when the person borrowing the money does not have a regular set income. But in this instance, that was fine. They gave Dad a loan for the full amount . . . and within half an hour, he and Kelly were traveling down the highway, heading northwest toward Kansas.

Mom joined them there within the week, and from there it was on to New Mexico and California.

And then, early on Father's Day morning of 1977, I received a frantic phone call from my Grandmother Donk, who told me that my family's house had burned to the ground during the night.

"But what . . . why . . . how . . . ?" I couldn't seem to focus my thoughts, but she knew what I was trying to ask.

"They don't know what caused it. Probably an electrical short of some kind. The house went up just like that. By the time the fire-trucks got there, there wasn't anything they could do."

"Oh no!" I dropped down onto the nearest chair so hard I almost broke it.

"Did they manage to save . . . ."

"No . . . I'm sorry. It's a total loss. Everything burned. Everything."

It was just before 7:00 o'clock in the morning, California time, when I called my parents to give them the news.

I wasn't sure if I'd even be able to find them, but I did

have a few numbers to try, and finally I got Dad on the phone.

I didn't know how to break the news.

"Good morning, Dad," I began. "And . . . uh . . . happy Father's Day."

"Herbie," he sighed, "I know you didn't call me this early in the morning just to wish me a happy Father's Day. What's up?"

"Well . . . I just got a call from home and . . . ."

"And what?"

"And the house burned down last night."

Two thousand miles away from home, Dad felt completely helpless. Everything he and Mom owned had been destroyed. All of their clothes. All of Kelly's clothes. Their furniture. All the family photos and keepsakes. And all of the records for CMA. Every single piece of paper pertaining to CMA was now nothing more than ashes.

What made it even worse was that there was no insurance. On top of that, he had just borrowed $3500 to buy a sidecar.

Even at that moment, though, there was no doubt but that God's hand was at work. According to the authorities, once the fire started, it spread through the house in a matter of minutes. Had Mom and Kelly been at home and asleep in their beds, they almost certainly would have died.

And so, even in the midst of his sorrow, Dad bowed his head and thanked God for sparing the lives of his wife and son.

Then he broke the news to Mom as gently as possible. He was surprised by the calm way she took it . . . without any apparent show of emotion.

Now they had to decide what to do.

"Mom," he said. "What do you think? You want to head for home?"

"No," she shook her head. "We've made commitments. We need to keep them. Besides, there's really nothing we can do. What's done is done."

They were due to leave the following day for Redding, several hundred miles to the north, where a large Retread Rally was being held.

That next week turned out to be an especially tough time for them. There was a wild group of people in Redding, and none of them seemed to be the least bit interested in Christianity. By the time Sunday morning came around, they were feeling particularly discouraged. The worship service had been relegated to a spot that was at least ten miles away from the rally, and it was scheduled at 6:30 in the morning. Even if people were willing to make the trip, Dad felt it was highly unlikely that any of them would be willing to get up that early on a Sunday—especially after the wild celebrating on Saturday night had continued into the middle of the night.

As they were getting ready to leave for the service, Dad reached over and pulled my mother close to him, "You know," he said, "I really don't know if anybody will be there except for you, me, Kelly and Ken. (Ken Sellars was a friend of my parents who came from Bisbee, Arizona to travel with them so he could provide the music for their services.)

She smiled and patted his hand.

"Well, at least we're here. And we'll have a chance to worship."

Something wonderful happened that morning.

Some of the seeds my folks had tried to plant that week had taken root after all. More than fifty people made the ten-mile trek to the service, and before it was over, twenty-one of them had professed faith in Christ.

Afterwards, Mom and Dad both wept over the way God

had honored their commitment to Him. Then they packed their few belongings—an extra pair of jeans apiece and a few shirts was all they had—and began the 2,000-mile ride back home.

It didn't really hit Mom that their home was gone until they were fifty miles or so away from Hatfield. That was when she had Dad pull over and had a good cry about all of the things she had lost. That was the first time my dad could remember her showing any emotion or pain related to the fire.

"It just came to me," she sobbed, "that we don't have anything to go home to."

"I know. I know." He held her for a few minutes, not knowing what to say.

After a brief cry, she had it out of her system and was ready to go on. She had just needed a few moments to grieve, and then she was fine.

Because they didn't have anywhere else to go, my folks moved into the CMA office building.

But, over the next few weeks, as word of their loss spread, money began to come in. Interestingly, much, or even most of it, came from non-Christians . . . people who appreciated what my parents were trying to do even if they didn't exactly share the vision or the commitment to the Lord.

By the time the money stopped coming, more than $18,000 had been sent, and in those days, in Arkansas, that was enough to rebuild. But that took more than a year, and all during that time, they lived in the office building, sleeping on mats on the floor.

During that year, the reputation of CMA continued to grow, and people from all over came to visit and find out more about this new organization.

Millionaires visited. Attorneys. Congressmen.

And if they stayed, as they often did, they, too, slept on the floor.

Truly, those were the hungry years of the Christian Motorcyclists Association. But through it all, the reputation and the witness of the CMA was growing stronger every day.

But as Mom and Dad were about to discover, not everyone was happy about that.

CHAPTER 9

Confrontation

It happened in Sturgis, South Dakota, during the summer of 1976.

Every summer, thousands of bikers from all over the United States and Canada converge on this small prairie town for a week of revelry, celebration, races, games, and hard, fast living. Sturgis might be considered the Mardi Gras for motorcyclists. Every one who rides has to make at least *one* pilgrimage to this huge event.

Now every year since 1976, CMA has been very much in evidence at Sturgis.

But that was the very first time CMA had even tried to present a Christian witness there, and nobody really knew what to expect.

The CMA group consisted of Mom, Dad, Kelly, and a handful of other members. They camped out together in City Park, which has since been closed to campers.

Mom had made a banner, which they hung in the trees over their little section of tents, just to let everyone know they were there. Actually, that banner had caused a little bit of friction between Mom and Dad, because things were so tight financially at the time, and Dad wasn't really sure that he wanted her to spend the money it took to make it.

But she insisted, so he gave in . . . and she made a beautiful banner. The very first day of the rally was enough to make Dad think that he shouldn't have brought Mom and

Kelly with him. All of the rallies they'd been to before were very small and tame in comparison to what went on here. But there was no turning back now.

That night, they went to bed early, tried to shut out all of the noise from the wild celebration that raged on around them, and finally drifted off to sleep.

It was after midnight when they were awakened by a chorus of drunken voices singing *Amazing Grace* just outside their tent.

At least that was the tune. The words had nothing at all to do with grace. They were perverse, obscene, and border-line threatening.

Dad got up and peeked outside. There were a dozen or so outlaws—big, hairy guys with tatoos—holding a mock church service underneath the CMA banner. Somewhere along the way, these men had been close enough to a church to learn several Christian songs. They knew the tunes to *Lord, I'm Coming Home,* and *Just As I Am,* but the words got more and more perverted as they went along— and the voices became more and more slurred.

Finally, they'd had enough of their fun, and stumbled off into the darkness to sleep it off.

Mom lay awake in her sleeping bag for a long time, shaking with a mixture of outrage and fear. The way these men had mocked her Lord made her feel sick inside. She was awake almost all night, and the next morning at breakfast she told the others that she wanted to go home.

"We don't belong here," she said. "We should just leave."

One of the other women tried to talk her out of it.

"No . . . we can't do that. Can't you see that that's exactly what they want us to do? Now, more than ever, we've *got* to stay here."

Mom had to admit that the other woman was right. This dark place desperately needed the light of Christ's love, but she still didn't feel good about being there—especially not with her little boy. She agreed that she would pray about it, and seek the Lord's will as to what they should do.

And as she did, the Lord directed her to the 91st Psalm. The entire Psalm is devoted to a discussion of God's protection of the righteous, and she took particular comfort from the ninth and tenth verses:

> *"If you make the Most High your dwelling—even the Lord who is my refuge—then no harm will befall you, no disaster will come near your tent."*

She knew that Scripture was a direct word from the Lord to her. And so, as difficult as it was, she agreed, that yes, they needed to stay at the rally and continue to be a witness for Christ.

The rest of the week was a challenge.

Every night, the outlaws held their mock service. They became increasingly more threatening. And they didn't seem like idle threats. They carried guns and knives . . . and who knew what they might do when they were drunk or stoned? They made it very clear that they didn't like Christians "interfering" with their "fun." The implied threats and verbal abuse were almost constant.

The worst of the lot was a guy known only as "Bear." He was one scary-looking dude, with an attitude to match his looks. Mom slept in her jeans every night during the rally, with her boots close at hand. She was prepared to run if and when she had to.

Still, in the middle of that type of madness, one of the outlaws, a guy named Roger, would sneak away just about every night to talk to Mom about the Lord. He was almost always drunk when he did so, but somewhere along the line in his life, he had known God, and it was when he was drunk that he most realized how far away from the Lord he had drifted. Some nights, he would get so drunk that he would pass out and sleep at the door to my parents' tent.

But they never complained. They never told him to leave them alone. Instead, they did their best to treat him with respect and show him the love of God.

During one of their conversations, Roger had asked Mom, "If your husband doesn't have a church, then how does he get paid?"

"Well, he doesn't really get paid," she said. "But you know . . . sometimes people will give us money . . . or take up an offering, or something like that. The Lord provides."

"The Lord provides?" He had tears in his eyes when he said it.

"You folks have given up a lot."

She shrugged. "Not really. This is what the Lord has called us to do. And there couldn't be anything better than doing what God wants you to do?"

"You people really love us, don't you?" He practically choked the words out.

"Yes, we do," my mother assured him. "We love you . . . and God loves you. Very much."

At that point, he walked away, too overcome to continue the conversation.

Roger was torn between two life-styles—but the seeds had been planted that would eventually see him surrender his life to Christ.

And then, came the final evening of the rally, and the big barbecue dinner provided by the city of Sturgis.

My folks had already taken their tents down, but they had left their banner up in case anybody wanted to find them at the dinner. And some people did want to find them. The same outlaws who had held the mock church service on the first night of the rally.

They came with their liquor and their beer kegs, and set everything up directly underneath my parents banner.

As they drank, they toasted the banner, "We drink in the name of Jesus," they would yell before chug-a-lugging their beer and whiskey.

Roger was there, too, drinking as usual, but at least he didn't seem to be joining in the mocking and the blasphemy.

But the others were having a great time.

"Here's to God!"

"Hey, guys," Bear shouted, in mock fear, "We'd better be careful. This is holy ground, you know. God might zap us all!"

They all thought that was terribly funny.

All through dinner that kind of behavior continued, while the little band of CMA members quietly ate nearby. Dad was angry, but he wasn't sure how the Lord wanted him to respond. So he was praying silently, "Lord, I know you want me to love these people, and I'm really struggling with that. Help me. And Lord . . . please forgive them, because I know it's you they're mocking. Not us."

After dinner was finished, he decided to go over and tell the outlaws that he wanted his banner back.

"Excuse me, but I . . . ."

"Yeah, Preacher," Bear spit out at him. "What do you want?"

"Just my banner."

"Oh, sure, Preach, you need your precious banner. Guess you gotta get home to your church, huh?"

"No," Dad shook his head. "I don't have a church."

"What do you mean you don't have a church. You can't be a preacher without a church?"

"Well, I guess I'm not a preacher then, because this is what I do."

Mom was standing nearby, and Bear nodded in her direction. "Hey, lady . . . your old man says he doesn't have a church. What's he talking about?"

"He's telling you the truth," she said. "He had a church, but he gave it up."

"He gave it up? Why the h— would he want to do something like that?"

"Because . . . he wanted to spend his time coming to rallies like this . . . and talking to guys like you . . . about Jesus."

The atmosphere changed immediately. The mocking, swaggering spirit seemed to evaporate.

After a long moment of quiet, Bear said, "Okay, Preacher. We'll get your banner for you."

He untied it, folded it neatly and handed it to Dad, who thanked him and started to put it into his pack.

A few minutes later, my folks were packed, loaded and ready to go. Mom and Kelly were in the sidecar, and Dad was just getting ready to get on his bike when Bear came running up.

"Hey, Preacher . . . Preacher!"

Dad stopped and waited.

"I was wondering if you could do me a big favor?"

"I'll try."

"Well . . . I was just hoping that . . . you might let me. . . . Could I have that banner?"

"You want the banner? What for?"

"I don't know. It just . . . it would mean a lot to me if you'd let me have it."

Dad looked at Mom. "Well . . . what do you think?"

She just smiled at him.

Dad sighed, "If you really want it . . . it's yours."

"Thank you. Thank you very much."

Dad reached in, got the banner out of his pack and handed it over.

"Do me a favor," he said. "Every time you look at this, you think about how much Jesus loves you, okay?"

"Oh, don't worry. I will."

Bear went off carrying the banner like it was something precious. Dad figured that the next time he got drunk he'd probably forget all about it—maybe even tear it up or lose it. But then again, you never know. It might have a profound effect on the guy's life.

My folks never saw Bear again. But some time later—two or three years later—they got a surprise package in the mail.

They opened it to find that banner inside, in perfect condition except for a few burn marks around one of the edges.

Inside, a hand-written note said:

> *Dear Friends,*
>
> *I hope you remember me. You gave me this banner at Sturgis a few years ago, and it's meant an awful lot to me. It would be hard to tell you exactly how much.*
>
> *Well, anyway, a few days ago, my house burned down, and I lost almost everything I had. But I did manage to save the banner. And I thought you might want it back.*
>
> *I'm trying to live for Jesus . . . but it's not always easy. Pray for me.*
>
> *Bear*

They were pleased to hear from him after all those years and to know that he was trying to live for God. When they had first arrived at Sturgis, Bear had seemed like the least likely prospect for conversion. His letter brought home once again that there is no barrier so great that it can hold back God's love.

Over the next several years, Dad averaged between 40,000 and 60,000 miles a year on his motorcycle. Sometimes he traveled alone. Other times he went with friends from CMA. But most of the time he traveled with Mom and Kelly—and Kelly was home-schooled along the way.

While Dad was traveling throughout North America, Diane and I were attending school at Arkansas Tech University. We had been able to get grants for tuition and books, and both of us were involved in a Work Study program on campus that paid enough for us to get a little apartment.

My plan was to major in pre-law, go on to law school, and then get into politics. Despite my negative attitude toward religion in general and God in particular, I did want to make the world a better place.

At least I had given up my plan to spend the rest of my life as an outlaw biker. Marriage had a way of changing your mind about such things. That, and the fact that I had the dubious thrill of meeting just such a biker when I was on that six-week cross-country trip with Dad.

I met him when we stopped to get gas at a little station somewhere in New Mexico. I was sitting on the curb outside drinking a soda when an honest-to-goodness outlaw came roaring up on his Harley Chopper, spewing a huge cloud of dust behind him. He looked to me like something out of a dream. Big. Muscular. Hairy. Tatoos. The whole bit. He was wearing his jacket, flying his colors, and I thought, "Oh, man! This is so cool!"

I watched with awe as he pumped some gas into his motorcycle, and then went inside to pay. He came out carrying a soda and—wonder of wonders—sat down right beside me.

It took me a minute to get up enough courage to speak to him, but I finally did, "Hey, where's the rest of your gang?"

"My gang?" He shrugged. "I don't know."

"But I thought you guys always rode together. What are you doing way out here all by yourself?"

He tipped up his bottle and drank it all in one long gulp. Then he sat there for a moment, just staring at the empty bottle.

Finally, he burped loudly, and then he spoke. "Aw . . . I don't know. Y'know . . . I'm just out here trying to get myself together. Trying to figure out what to do with my life . . . . I'm just trying to find myself."

I couldn't believe it. What did he mean by that? He had already "found" himself. What could there possibly be that was better than riding wild and free on a motorcycle, doing whatever you wanted to do whenever you wanted to do it?

That day, I was disillusioned, and the dream of becoming an outlaw lost more than a little bit of its luster.

I've thought about that guy a lot over the years, and wondered if God sent him just to talk to me. Perhaps he was an angel? Whatever the case, I'll always be glad I met him.

Anyway, while we were attending school, Diane and I went to church on Sunday because Diane wanted to go. But otherwise, I wasn't much interested in religious matters. Diane knew that I had a bad attitude where God was concerned, but she really didn't know the depth of it.

We attended a little Missionary Baptist Church for several weeks before we finally asked to be accepted as members —something that required a vote of the entire congregation.

We were required to stand up front on a Sunday morning, while the pastor asked the members of the congregation whether they wanted to accept us. He took us one at a time, Diane first, and when he brought her name before the congregation there was immediate, unanimous approval.

Then, it was my turn. This time, the response wasn't quite so enthusiastic. In fact, nobody said anything. I stood in front of the congregation for a full two minutes, feeling my face turning a deeper red with every second that passed— because there was nothing but silence. Everyone sat there looking at me and my long hair in particular. Nobody said a word.

Finally, I *was* accepted into the church, but clearly, it was only because I was Diane's husband. Otherwise, forget it!

Naturally, that only added to the resentment I felt toward Christians. But Diane still kept taking me to church, and hoping that something I'd hear or see there would make an impact on me.

It didn't.

But a relationship with a couple of the guys I worked with did.

They were totally different from any other Christians I'd ever known. For one thing, they had long hair like me. They listened to Christian rock music, which I discovered was pretty cool. But the best thing about them was that they were good guys—they worked hard, but they knew how to have a good time, and they were fun to be around.

They weren't playing at Christianity either. They both believed deeply in God, and sometimes on their breaks, I'd see them reading their Bibles. Everything about them impressed me. For a long time, I watched them to see if they would do anything "wrong," but they never did. And so my admiration and respect for both of them just kept growing.

I liked to talk to them about what they believed and why, even arguing with them about the existence of God. They always had answers to my questions and my challenges. Actually, I was glad about that. I *wanted* them to know how to handle the tough questions I threw at them. I *wanted* them to convince me that they were right about God. And they were doing a very good job of it.

Now, at the same time I was getting to know these two guys—Chris and Robert—there was another guy in the cafeteria who was a complete royal pain in the neck.

I don't remember his name—only that we called him "Red," and Red was a karate expert.

And he wasn't the least bit shy when it came to letting you know about it. He was forever throwing shadow punches or kicks at whoever happened to be within range.

"Whap!" He'd throw a punch at you, stopping within an inch or so of your nose. "Man . . . one more inch and I could have killed you!"

Or he'd throw a kick at your groin, again stopping just in time.

And it wasn't just me. He did it to everybody. If he wasn't "demonstrating" how he could injure you, he was talking about his prowess in karate. He was especially annoying when you were working in line in the cafeteria, trying to serve food, and he was showing off, constantly slapping and kicking at you.

The Christian guys seemed to take it all in stride. It was obvious they didn't like it, but they did their best to put up with his behavior.

Sometimes they'd try to reason with him, "Why do you do this? Don't you know that people aren't going to like you?"

His reaction was always the same, "Who cares?"

Sometimes I'd get so mad I'd say, "One of these days, I'm gonna haul off and punch that guy in the mouth."

"Oh, let it roll off of you," Chris would say. "He just needs attention. He probably doesn't have any friends and he feels insecure."

"He's got a great way of making friends!" I fumed.

I knew I wasn't going to be able to take much more of it.

Now it's hard to put up with someone who's always putting his fist in your face. But it's almost impossible to put up with it at six in the morning. And that's when I finally exploded.

We were just starting to get ready for the breakfast crowd when Red waltzed up, took a karate stance, and kicked his foot into my face, stopping just in front of my eyes.

"Listen," I said, "You're not the only one here who knows karate. And if you ever do that again, I'm going to bust your head."

He looked at me as if I'd lost my mind.

"Oooooh," he said, "looks like we've got some competition, here."

And then he twisted around and kicked his foot into my face a second time.

The truth was that I really didn't know karate at all. I knew all of one punch, and that was it. But I was mad enough to use it. I pushed his foot out of my face and hit him right under the nose, twisting my fist as I did so. I hit him with such force that I busted his nose. Caught by surprise, he fell backwards, first hitting his back on the corner of a table, then smashing his head on a shelf, and winding up unconscious on the floor.

As I stood over him, my first thought was, "Oh, no! What have I done?" This guy *really* knew karate, and I figured that when he regained consciousness, he was probably going to kill me.

Of course, everyone back in the kitchen saw what I had done, and they erupted into a round of applause. Everybody *wanted* to punch Red, and they were happy that somebody had finally done it.

As Red started to come to, I figured I'd better continue

the bluff, so I took up a karate stance—or something that I figured at least *looked* like a karate stance—and said, "Don't you ever do that again . . . or I'll finish it."

Instead of attacking me, Red limped out of the room to take care of his wounds, and my status as a hero was confirmed. By the end of the day, the story of what I had done had grown until Red and I had engaged in some kind of a "Karate Kid"-type brawl. Everyone was congratulating me and thanking me for putting Red in his place.

The only thing I was worried about was what my Christian friends would think. I knew they weren't going to like the fact that I had resorted to violence. The fact that I was worried about what they might think shows how much I had come to respect them.

And, sure enough, Chris came up to me around lunchtime.

"Hey, I heard what you did to Red."

"Yeah . . . well . . . he just pushed me too far."

He sighed and nodded. "I know . . . I wish it could have been handled another way. But sometimes, that's just not possible." Then he patted me on the back.

"Maybe it's not very Christian of me. But, I want you to know that I'm proud of you!"

I can't tell you what that meant to me. He hadn't put me down, or lectured me, or told me that Jesus wouldn't approve of what I had done. It's impossible for me to tell you how much that meant to me.

As for Red, he didn't come back to work the rest of the day, but when he finally did come back, he was different. Not only different, but better. He didn't go around throwing karate punches all the time. In fact, he turned out to be kind of a regular, likeable guy. He didn't have to go around anymore pretending to be Mr. Karate King, and that was good for him. Punching him in the nose was probably the best thing I could have done for him!

It was about that time that *Helter Skelter*, a movie on the life of killer Charles Manson was broadcast over one of the television networks, and that movie was the number one topic of conversation at the cafeteria the next day.

One of the guys in the chow line said, "Man . . . that Manson guy was really crazy. He thought he was Jesus."

In typical smart-guy fashion, someone else shot back, "Well, how do you know he *wasn't* Jesus?"

Well, that was a stupid question. I knew Charles Manson wasn't Jesus. But I couldn't for the life of me say *why* he wasn't Jesus. But my friend Chris had an immediate answer.

"Because," he said, "Jesus is in my heart. And the Jesus who lives in my heart isn't anything like Charles Manson." He said it so fast. It was really an impulse reaction, and it was obvious that Chris was speaking the truth.

He knew that Charles Manson couldn't be Jesus Christ because he had a personal relationship with the *real* Jesus, and the depth of that relationship could be seen in the look on his face and heard in the tone of his voice.

And I thought, "Wow! I really wish I knew Jesus the way he does."

And so, that night after Diane was asleep, I got out of bed and took my Bible into the bathroom, where I read for hours. As strange as it seems, I'd never really read the Bible before, at least not the way I read it now. For the first time, I was "searching the Scriptures" to see if they were true. And, the more I read, the more it seemed to me that they *had* to be true.

This went on for several nights. I'd sit on the side of the bathtub and read and pray that God would reveal himself to me. I had decided that if I couldn't find meaning in the Christian Scriptures, I would set them aside forever, and look for meaning in another direction—perhaps the eastern mysticism which was so popular then.

"God," I prayed, "I can't believe in you because my folks do . . . or because Diane does . . . or because Chris does. I've got to believe in You for myself. You've got to be real to me!"

One night as I was reading, I came to a passage where Jesus said, "Verily, I say, the works I do, you shall do . . ." and ". . . whatsoever you ask in my name, I will do it." That portion of Scripture just leaped off the page and I thought, "Wow! Wouldn't it be great if this were true?"

The next day at breakfast, as Diane and I were sitting at our little dinette table eating cereal, I decided to tell her what I'd been doing.

"Diane . . . every night, after you're asleep, I've been getting out of bed and . . . ."

Her spoon fell into her cereal bowl with a splash. "Oh, no! Where have . . ."

"No, no, wait. It's nothing like that." I reached over and took her hand. "I've been going into the bathroom, and reading the Bible."

"The bathroom? Well . . . I'm glad you're reading the Bible. But why . . ."

"Because I don't want you messing with me, that's why." She looked hurt.

"Please . . . don't feel bad, Diane. It's just that I want to read it for myself. I want to make up my own mind. I don't want anybody helping me or telling me what it means."

She smiled that beautiful smile that always makes me fall in love with her all over again every time I see it.

"That's great, Herbie. Really great . . . So, are you enjoying it?"

"Oh, yeah, I am. But some of it confuses me." I got up to pour myself a second cup of coffee.

"Like last night, I was reading where Jesus said that if we believe in Him, we should be able to do the same works He did."

"Uh huh—John 14:12."

"Yeah. Well, do you believe that?"

"Of course I do!" (Diane knew that I was probably taking the verse more than a wee bit too literally, but at this point she was just excited that I was reading the Bible and didn't want to engage in any theological debates with me!)

"Well then . . . do you understand what that means? Just think about it! I mean that's so exciting!"

"It certainly is!"

I thought about that verse all day. And the more I thought about it, the more excited I got. I felt that I was the only one who knew that particular verse was in there. After all, if other people knew about it, they'd be every bit as excited as I was . . . wouldn't they?

At that time, we were still attending the little Missionary Baptist Church, and every Wednesday night at the midweek prayer service, the pastor would start off by asking for testimonies from members of the congregation. I'm sure the testimonies were supposed to be a source of encouragement and excitement, but they usually had the opposite effect on me. And no wonder. The "testimonies" usually went something like this:

"I just praise God that I'm not dead yet."

Or, "I've been in terrible, terrible pain, but I praise God anyway, because He's been with me."

Or, "Well, my dog died this week, but I thank the Lord that I've still got my cat."

They weren't the sort of testimonies that made a person want to jump and shout for joy.

But on this particular night, I was ready when the preacher asked for testimonies. I was going to do something to add a little bit of life and enthusiasm to these proceedings.

"Yes . . . I have something I want to share!"

"That's great, Herbie. What is it?"

I stood up and said, "Listen. You gotta hear this!"

Of course, I was wearing my jeans and leathers, which is what I wore almost all the time, so some of the people weren't inclined to pay a whole lot of attention to anything I said, even if it did come straight out of the Bible.

I turned to the 14th chapter of John and excitedly read the passage I had discovered the night before. There were a lot of people there, and because I was nervous, I stumbled a few times.

When I was finished, I looked around expectantly. I don't know what I thought would happen. At the very least, I figured they'd be opening up their Bibles, anxious to read that portion of scripture for themselves. I certainly expected *some* show of interest or excitement.

Instead, they sat there looking at me with the same disinterested, pathetic expressions on their faces.

I cleared my throat.

"I think . . . maybe I read that wrong. Let me read it again."

This time I read slower, with more feeling, and when I had finished I looked around and said, "Did you get that?"

Still no reaction.

I looked at the preacher, who smiled and said, with more than a hint of condescension in his voice, "That was nice, Herbie. Very nice. Thank you for sharing that with us." Then he went on to the next "testimony."

I sat there feeling confused and defeated.

As Diane and I were climbing on our motorcycle after the service that night, I asked her what had gone wrong. "Did I read that right."

"You read it great!"

"But what happened then? That's so exciting, and they just sat there . . . like statues."

Diane sighed.

"Well, I think that maybe they've read that before. And they've just kind of gotten used to what it says."

That hit me hard.

"I hope," I said, as I pulled my helmet on, "that I'll never get used to what the Bible says."

"Me neither," she replied, as I gunned the motorcycle into gear and we headed off into the night.

Over the next few days it was obvious to me, and to everyone who knew me, that something had changed in my life. I was just different.

I went to Chris and told him I needed to talk to him.

"You might find this hard to believe," I told him. "But I grew up in a pastor's home. My dad's an evangelist."

"Really?"

"Yeah . . . that's true. But I've never known Jesus the way you do. And I want to. I want to know more about Him. I want to have Him in my life the way you have Him in yours."

"Praise the Lord! This is wonderful."

Although I had heard God's plan of salvation many times before, when Chris explained it to me, it was like it was brand new. And suddenly, it all made complete, perfect sense.

That day, I decided that I didn't want to spend anymore time standing on the outside looking in. Walking along the campus after my first class that morning, I told God that when Sunday came, I would surrender my life to Him. But as soon as I said it, I knew I couldn't wait that long. I'd have to do it now. Right now!

I turned in the direction of our apartment and quickened my pace. When I got home, I was happy to discover that Diane was gone. That was because I knew I needed some time to be alone with God. I fell to my knees in front of a big, overstuffed orange chair.

"Jesus," I cried, "I'm surrendering my life to you right now. Please, Lord, use me any way you see fit."

Suddenly, the faces of those six men I had hated for so long filled my mind. I knew that I had only been hurting myself by carrying that hurt and anger with me all these years.

"Lord Jesus," I prayed. "I forgive those men. Please, take away my bitterness and give me love for them. Jesus . . . I surrender everything to you. My life. My marriage. Everything!" I kept on praying, pouring out my heart, confessing every sin I had ever committed—or at least every one I could remember.

I don't know how long I prayed, but it was the most wonderful, cleansing experience of my life.

For the first time in my life, I knew the meaning of a father's love. For the first time in my life, I was willing to *accept* a father's love. I wept as I realized how much God loved me. How much Dad loved me. I wept because I knew the prodigal had come back home.

And then I wept because I thought of all the other prodigals. All those thousands who, like me, had turned their backs on God because they thought He didn't care. As wave after wave of His love washed over me and through me, I thought about how very wrong they were. How very wrong I had been. I understood now why Dad wouldn't let anything stop him from doing everything in his power to tell the lost about the love of Christ—and I knew that from that day forward, I would feel exactly the same way.

RIDING THE CROSSROADS

When I got up off my knees, I was a new creature in Jesus.

But there was one pressing question, "What was I supposed to do next?"

CHAPTER 10

On the Road Again

I don't know, really, what I thought Dad would do when I told him about the way Christ had come into my life. What I didn't expect was for him to take the news with a calm smile, but that's exactly what he did.

He was thrilled, yes. He was pleased, absolutely. But he wasn't a bit surprised. It was almost as if he expected it to happen—and I suppose he did. After all, he knew I couldn't keep running from God's love forever.

Out there on the road, he was discovering anew every day that there is no way you can possibly overestimate the width of God's love, grace or mercy. God's love is the greatest power in the universe, and Dad was seeing that truth demonstrated every day, as bikers and motorcyclists all across America were being swept gently into His kingdom. He knew all along that it was only a matter of time before that love took me in.

As I was just starting out in the Christian life—taking baby steps—CMA was spreading out all over the country. There were more than 1,000 members by June of 1978, and dozens of new memberships were arriving every month.

God began the process of bringing into the organization people who loved Him with all their hearts, souls and minds . . . people who had the skills and the expertise to take the organization past the initial "mom and pop" stage of its infancy.

RIDING THE CROSSROADS

People such as Roy and June Johnson, Tom and Phyllis Pittman, Greg Heinritz, Curtis Clements . . . .

The Johnsons were cotton farmers who lived with their two children just outside of Lubbock, Texas.

Their membership application was actually the last one to arrive before my parents' home burned, and their records were destroyed in the fire. Somehow, though, Mom was able to remember their address and was able to let them know what had happened.

(My mother wrote as many people as she could track down, although there was no way she could have contacted all of those whose records were lost.)

Roy Johnson was delighted when he heard about CMA because he was a long-time Christian *and* a long-time motorcyclist.

He had first begun riding way back in 1940, on an Indian 45 with a Scout frame. He took time out for a stint in the Navy, but then went back to his motorcycle after the war. He met June, married her, and, sometime in the late 1950s, talked her into taking up motorcycling herself.

June wasn't thrilled with motorcycling at first, but she "learned to love it," and soon they were going on long trips together. They had both come to the Lord when they were young, and they were both very committed to Him, so witnessing was a natural part of their lives.

The first rally they attended where CMA had a visible presence was in Kerrville, Texas, and they were so impressed by what they heard that they decided to ride all the way to Sierra Vista, Arizona, to attend another rally. From there, they rode with Dad and some other cyclists up into Northern Arizona and on into New Mexico. And they have been active participants in CMA ever since.

Roy knew a lot about farming, and he spent a lot of time

learning about computers and how they could assist with the growth and organization of CMA.

It wasn't long before Roy was asked to become a CMA area representative for West Texas and, in 1978, June took over as secretary/treasurer for the national organization. At that time, CMA's business office was moved into their home, where it stayed until 1994, then it was finally moved into the national headquarters in Arkansas.

Roy is in his 70's now, but he's still out there, putting the miles on his motorcycle.

Tom Pittman is a long-time friend of Dad's. The two of them went to school together, and, in fact, Dad's dad was his spiritual father.

Tom came from a rough background, and when Jesus came into his life, He did so in a dramatic, mighty way. Everyone who knew Tom knew that something great had happened to him. The change was so startling.

He went on to be a preacher and pastor, a tremendously effective soul winner.

Tom Pittman left the pulpit to become CMA's second full-time staff member—Dad being the first. It wasn't easy for him at first, because he was not used to being out on the road all the time—especially on a motorcycle. But he persevered, sure of God's calling on his life, and there is no telling how many people he has led to the Lord as he's traveled the highways and byways over the years.

Greg Heinritz was a millionaire by the time he was 18, and not because he inherited a fortune. He is a brilliant, hard-working man, who saved his money and invested it wisely. But he had a problem maintaining his investment.

During one especially cold winter, many thousands of dollars worth of underground pipes froze and burst throughout the United States, and, as Greg said, "I think I owned every one of those pipes."

In that one, short winter, he lost everything. He had to spend his last $30,000 just to go bankrupt.

Then, he got on his bike and headed to Arizona, where he hoped to rescue his brother from a "cult" that had brainwashed him.

But Greg's brother hadn't joined a cult. He had become a born-again Christian, and he convinced Greg that he, too, needed to give his life to Christ.

Now, Greg had paid several thousand dollars to get his motorcycle painted up with pornographic pictures.

But after Greg got saved, he wasn't so proud of that bike anymore. In fact, when he rode it to a CMA rally, he hid it in the bushes outside the area, rather than riding it right into the middle of activities, as he usually did. And then, after listening to the messages from the CMA evangelist that day, Greg decided that he could no longer ride that bike looking the way it did. So he got a can of spray paint, and covered up all those pornographic (and expensive) paintings with grey primer!

Later on, Greg was to become a full-time evangelist for CMA, and he had his motorcycle re-painted, this time with Christian imagery.

You may have seen photos of it, because, at one time, it was the most photographed motorcycle in the world.

Curtis Clements was a policeman in Dallas for years—and he was also a man consumed by thoughts of revenge. One day while driving in the city of Dallas, Curtis' son was shot and seriously injured by another motorist.

Curtis was driven by the desire to personally see that the man who had hurt his son would pay with his own life.

That wasn't the way it worked out, however. Instead, Curtis was in a horrible motorcycle accident. He was almost killed, and had to spend weeks in the hospital recovering from his injuries. His injuries were so severe that his entire face had to be rebuilt.

It was while he was languishing in that hospital bed that the Lord touched him, and he was set free from the grief, anger and bitterness he had carried for so long. Clements left the hospital a changed man. Soon thereafter, he heard about a new organization called CMA . . . and he and his wife quickly became active in the organization as lay evangelists. Later, he became a full-time staff member.

There are so many men and women who helped to build CMA into what it is today, and these are just a few of them.

During those days, God was definitely doing a great work in the life of the Christian Motorcyclists Association.

And he was doing some pretty good things in my life, too.

Shortly after I had committed my life to Christ, Diane and I started a weekly Bible study in our apartment. I was up front about my lack of biblical knowledge. I told people that if they were expecting me to be an authority on the Scriptures, they were going to be sorely disappointed. I told them that I didn't really consider myself to be a teacher. But I thought it would be terrific if we could all learn together.

The embarrassing truth was that I didn't even know the order of the books of the Bible. And so, when I wrote out my plan for the Bible study every week, I not only wrote down book, chapter and verse, but page number as well. It's amazing that someone who had spent so much time in church could have been so ignorant about the Bible—but it proves that if a person isn't really interested in learning, he won't learn.

Thankfully, Diane was there to back me up when I needed it, and she *did* know the Bible. I was amazed by how much she knew and how much insight she had.

But what I lacked in knowledge, I made up for in enthusiasm. I wasn't shy about inviting people to our weekly meetings, and many of them responded. Our Bible study got off to a booming start and grew from there.

Within a few weeks, so many people were coming that our little apartment could barely contain them. I learned from first-hand experience during those terrific days what it meant to be "packed like sardines." And yet, despite the uncomfortable, crowded conditions, people seemed to love those meetings, and hardly a week went by without at least one decision for Christ.

I remember in particular a young man from Saudi Arabia, who was led to the Lord in our parking lot by people who attended our prayer group. He was so happy when he found out how much God loved him!

He was from a wealthy, aristocratic Moslem family, and he had been instructed from the Koran from an early age. But that book and its teachings had left him longing for something more, something he had found in Jesus.

He knew that when he went back home, his family would disown him because of his "rejection" of Mohammed. By accepting Jesus as his Lord and Savior, he was, in fact, turning his back on an inheritance of several million dollars. He was also giving up a promising career as an engineer in his native land. But he was willing to give up everything for the sake of Christ.

You can imagine how that affected me. I had grown up hearing the Gospel preached almost every day of my life, but I hadn't responded. And here was a young man who had never even heard the story of Jesus until he reached college age, and now he was giving up *everything* for the sake of the Gospel.

How I regretted all the years I had thrown away in anger and bitterness. I vowed that there would be no more wasted years!

I began to think seriously about going into the ministry, full-time.

I was sitting at the dining table one day doing my homework, when I decided to "test the waters" with Diane.

"Diane," I said, "I've been thinking . . . ."

"Oh, oh," she teased. "Sounds dangerous."

"It might be!" I shot back. "But seriously, you know, I've just been feeling more and more like God is calling me into the ministry . . ."

"Really?"

Diane couldn't believe what she was hearing. All those years she had prayed that God would give her a minister for a husband, and now it looked like He was going to do it, in His own way and His own time.

"Well . . . it would mean we'd have to go to Bible School, and there'd be other changes . . ."

"Herbie! You know I'll do whatever it takes."

"Well, I've been thinking about it a lot, and it seems to me that if you really want to make this world a better place, you can't do it through politics."

"So you're giving up on politics?"

I snapped my book shut and leaned back in my chair.

"Politics isn't the answer. But when you bring someone into a personal relationship with God . . . . When a man gets saved, it affects his wife, his children, his co-workers and everyone he comes in contact with. His world is changed. And that's how you can change the world!"

As it turned out, Diane, too, had felt that God was calling me—or really, I should say "us"—into the ministry, but she didn't want to put any pressure on me. She knew it had to be my decision.

When we went home for the Christmas holidays, I told Mom and Dad that I felt that God was calling me to preach. I expected them to be excited, but they didn't seem to be.

At least, Dad wasn't. He told me that it was something between me and the Lord. Like Diane, he wanted it to be my decision. But he did have one suggestion.

At this time, Dad was back to pastoring a small church near Hatfield in addition to traveling the country for CMA. Sadly, his heart was acting up again, and he was facing more surgery, almost immediately.

"How would you like to fill in for me while I'm in the hospital?" he asked.

"Would that be okay?"

"It would be great! The experience might give you a better idea of whether this is really what God is calling you to do."

And so, over the next few days, as he was preparing to go back into the hospital, he spent as much time as possible teaching me how to put together and deliver an effective sermon.

With Dad's help, I wrote up a sermon that I figured would last anywhere from 30 to 45 minutes. But I must have been talking faster than Donald Duck when I finally stood up behind that pulpit, because I delivered the entire sermon in just under fifteen minutes. I couldn't believe how fast the time went!

Nevertheless, the Lord used what I said, and when the invitation was given, two teenaged girls came forward to say they wanted to accept Christ.

This was something I hadn't planned on. I had no idea what to do. Finally, I called one of the deacons to take them back into one of the Sunday School classes and talk to them. I knew how to lead people to the Lord in the familiar confines of my own apartment, but I wasn't exactly sure how to do it in front of the whole church. Oh, well. I would learn.

I don't know how good that first sermon was. But Diane,

bless her heart, made me feel like I was one step away from being the next Billy Graham. Others complimented me, too. They were gracious and appreciated the length.

Meanwhile, even though Dad's surgery went well, he wasn't going to be able to be back in the pulpit for at least another week, so he asked if I would fill in for him again the following Sunday.

This time, at the end of the invitation, I stepped down from the pulpit and said, "I really don't know how to do this, but I guess I'm surrendering my life to preach."

That day, it became definite. At the end of the semester— and three haircuts later—Diane and I would transfer to Baptist Christian College, in Shreveport, Louisiana, where I could get a degree in ministry.

Well, I learned an awful lot at Baptist Christian. And I worked very, very hard. I worked so hard, in fact, that I just about lost touch with God. In addition to my full load of courses, I worked a full-time job at the bank, and as a janitor at the school during the night hours. Diane and I also cleaned a number of churches at nights and on weekends in order to make ends meet.

My last semester there I took 21 hours of class work *and* worked two full-time jobs and several part-time jobs to help us get by. And every hour I worked was absolutely necessary. By the time we finished at Baptist Christian, our two oldest sons, Jeff and Randy, had been born and our third son, Benji, was on the way. And let me tell you, it was a struggle to keep those hungry guys fed!

I still loved God, but I was so busy trying to prepare myself so I could go out and be His servant, that I didn't have a whole lot of time for Him. When I had time to think about it, I missed the passion and excitement of my early days as a Christian. I missed those spiritually charged prayer meetings that had taken place in our apartment at Arkansas

Tech. But when I talked to my professors about my current lack of passion, they assured me that it was all part of the normal Christian walk. You couldn't expect that early fervency to last forever. I didn't like that very much, but I was happy to know, at least, that what I was going through was nothing out of the ordinary for any Christian.

Still, in many ways, our years at Baptist Christian were good ones. I became grounded in the Scriptures, and I was able to sit at the feet of many godly men and women, learning from their knowledge of the Scriptures and their years of experience. I had a good relationship with my professors and dean, and especially with the dean of students, Dr. Larry Gilliam. And even though my usual wardrobe reflected my "normal" working role as a janitor there at the school, if they needed to shine somebody up and send him out to represent the school, they very often chose me. I liked that. It meant that, by God's grace, I had come a very long way from the rebellious young man with long hair whose life's ambition was to fly the colors of an outlaw motorcycle gang.

I was even accorded the honor of being one of the few students asked to preach from the pulpit of the college church.

And so it was that, as the date for my graduation came around, I was summoned to the office of the school's president, Dr. Jimmy Tharpe. Dean Gilliam was there, along with a couple of other faculty members, and I had no idea what to expect.

When I got there, they were all smiling, so I knew it was something pretty good.

Dr. Gilliam took the lead.

"Herbie . . . have you decided what you're going to do after graduation?"

"Well, yes, sir. I want to preach."

He nodded. "I know. But I mean . . . do you have any immediate plans? Do you know where you're going to go?"

"Not really . . . I just figured . . . ."

President Tharpe interrupted me before I could finish.

"Herbie . . . we called you here because we'd like for you to stay on as assistant dean of students."

He went on to tell me that what they wanted to do was create a new position, especially for me. And although this wasn't exactly the way they put it, I got the definite feeling that the main reason they wanted me to stay around was because I was one of very few ministry students who could walk into the athletic dorm without being harassed!

In other words, the ministry students and the athletes got along about as well as cats and mice do.

For the most part, the ministry students were the stereotypical "spiritual" type. Scholarly . . . serious . . . intense.

Many of the athletes—who came to the school to play basketball or football—were the type who liked to beat up *that* type!

But it seemed I was different. I spent a lot of time in the athletic dorm just shooting the breeze with the guys. I had even participated in some of their dorm wrestling tournaments. They didn't even seem to mind that I wanted to talk about the Lord sometimes.

"Herbie," Dr. Tharpe said. "We need somebody like you."

I was excited by their offer and didn't have to think twice before saying yes. I served as assistant dean of students for a year, but it didn't take that long to decide that this wasn't really what God had called me to do. He wanted me to preach. And so, as soon as that first year was up, I turned in my resignation.

I didn't have any job offers. I didn't know where we were

going to go. And with a wife and a growing family, it was not an easy thing to give up a secure position. But Diane and I both felt that God was telling us to move on, and that He would take care of us.

We wound up in New Braunfels, Texas, and we began to pray fervently for God to grant us five good men to serve as the founding members of the church we hoped to build.

We also decided, after praying about it, that I should not get an additional job to support us. If God was calling me to be a minister, then that's what I would do. So we put up some flyers, made some door-to-door visits, and began having services on Sunday morning. I also began keeping regular office hours and spending my full-time tending to evangelism and other church "business," even though Diane and I and our boys sometimes made up nearly half of the attendance on Sunday morning. And with the kind of offerings we were getting, we certainly weren't going to have to worry about tax shelters or annuities. We must have come up with 47 different ways to fix Spam, and that's the only way we made it through those first few weeks in the ministry.

We were discovering that obedience wasn't always that easy. I was tempted more than once to go out and look for a part-time job. But I knew that wasn't what God wanted me to do, and I was determined to submit my will to His. And God was faithful. He quickly provided the five men we had prayed for. And then the next five. And then five after that. And so on. Before long, we had grown to the point where we needed a bigger place to hold our services. We needed a building of our own.

Driving around town, I came across an old country club that was on the market. It had seen better days, but it wasn't in the worst condition. The property consisted of several hillside acres, and, best of all, it had a building that would make a perfect sanctuary. But when I called a meeting of the leaders and told them that I thought we should try to buy the property, they all started looking at their calendar watches to see if perhaps it was April 1. It wasn't, and I wasn't fooling.

"But Herbie," one of them said. "We don't have any money? We can't buy a place like that."

"I'd like to try," I said. I'd seen enough by now to know that nothing was impossible with God.

"Well sure," he laughed, "we can try. But I think we should be prepared to have them laugh in our faces!"

He was right.

I called for a meeting with the owner of the property and his attorney and told them we wanted to buy the property for our church.

"That's fine," said the agent, pulling out his notebook. "What are you proposing?"

I looked him straight in the eye, just so he would know how serious I was. Actually, I think I was doing a bit more than that. I was calling on the old "bluffing technique" I had used in my younger days of running with the rough crowd. I was trying to look as calm, cool and collected as possible, but I was shaking inside.

"We'll give you $5,000 down," I told him. "And then, I'll give you five sealed envelopes—one each for the next five years. Inside each, there will be a receipt for a tax write-off of $5,000."

They just looked at me, so I went on.

"And, then, in addition, we'll give you $10,000 a year for five years."

The attorney looked like he had just discovered that I was wearing one of those water-squirting rubber flowers in my lapel.

After the initial shock wore off, he threw back his head

and laughed. "Five thousand dollars and tax write-offs? Son, . . . you can't buy this property for that!"

But then he noticed that his client wasn't laughing. The old man's eyes were twinkling, as if he were fighting the impulse to laugh, but instead, he reached out and put his hand on his attorney's arm.

"You know," he said. "I really like this young man's grit." The attorney stopped laughing.

"I want you to draw up the papers." He stood up and reached his hand out to me. "Preacher, you've got yourself a deal."

I'm certain that the attorney thought I had just pulled off the heist of the century. But the truth was that I was taking a giant leap of faith. We didn't *have* $5,000, and even if we could raise that much, there was no guarantee that we'd ever be able to come up with anything more. It was all we could do to cover expenses. Besides, many of our members were new Christians who hadn't learned to trust God in their giving.

Nevertheless, the following Sunday morning, I stood before the people and told them what had happened. I asked everyone to dig down deep and give sacrificially.

As the offering plate went down each aisle, the men from that aisle would get up and follow it to the next aisle. By the time the plate got to the last row, every man in the church was crowded around it, and together, they carried it into the back room to count the money.

A few minutes later, the church treasurer came back in, her face flushed with excitement, to give us the good news. The morning's offering was slightly more than $5,000! The entire congregation erupted into prolonged applause. We had our building!

Over the next weeks and months, our attendance seemed to grow more by multiplication than addition. The members of that church were on fire for God, and they worked hard to bring their friends and neighbors into the kingdom. As an example of the evangelical fervor that ran totally through that congregation, over a one-year period, our youth group *alone* was responsible for bringing more than 300 people into a personal relationship with Christ, and many of those became members of our church. It was not uncommon to see boys who were twelve or thirteen years old walking down the aisle holding the arms of men they'd led to the Lord. I remember one man in his seventies who told me, "I've had many people talk to me about Christ, but when that little boy rang my doorbell and said, 'Mister, do you know Jesus?' I just broke. I knew I couldn't resist the Lord any longer."

Much of our congregation was made up of new Christians, and many of them had been through some very tough times. Some had been addicted to drugs. Some were recovering alcoholics. Some had served time in jail. Some had been married three and four times.

Almost all of them had been lifted out of some very unpleasant circumstances by God's love and were proof of the biblical teaching that the one who has been forgiven much loves much.

I remember one time when I went to talk to some people about the Lord. As soon as they opened the door in response to my knock, I was almost overcome by the marijuana smoke.

Taking a step back, I said, "I've come to tell you about Jesus . . . but I don't think this is a good day. So I'm going to come back tomorrow night, and I want you to be straight."

They could have told me to drop dead, but they didn't. And when I did go back the next night, they were straight, and I led the entire family—the father, mother and their teenage son—to the Lord. They became dedicated followers of Christ and loyal, faithful members of our congregation.

Our explosive growth came despite the fact that our evangelistic style could be pretty rigid at times. We did not believe in anything called "cheap grace," and we were upfront about the fact that living the Christian life wasn't always a bed of roses.

When people came down the aisle at one of our services and said they wanted to surrender their lives to Christ, our response was always something like, "Are you serious about this, or are you playing games with God?"

If the answer was, "I'm serious," which it almost always was, then we would assign someone from the congregation to meet with them every day during the next week for a 45-minute Bible study. The second week, the Bible study would be 45 minutes every other day. The third week, the Bible study was to be held every third day, and then, after that, it would be once a month . . . forever.

Despite that rather hard stance, our growth continued to be phenomenal, and we received quite a bit of recognition as one of the fastest growing churches in Texas.

During my years as a pastor, I was connected to the Christian Motorcyclists Association in a number of ways.

Of course, I kept in touch with what the organization was doing through my relationship with Dad, which had never been better. I understood now about his passion for reaching lost souls, and I was proud of what he was accomplishing in and through CMA.

He was still on the road almost all of the time in those days, and Mom was usually with him. Kelly was a teenager now, and so he wasn't on the road as much, but he still went along more than occasionally. He was enrolled in a Christian school that allowed him to miss as much school as necessary, just as long as he took his assignments with him and kept up with his studies. It wasn't easy, but he managed to do it. In reality, Kelly was on the road with Dad far more than I ever was, and he was much more involved in the initial birth and growth of the Christian Motorcyclists Association.

Once in awhile, I would return to Hatfield to conduct seminars in evangelism for CMA members, and I always enjoyed that. Dad often asked me to think about coming to work for CMA full-time, but I always turned him down. It wasn't that I didn't love CMA, or that I had lost my passion for motorcycles. The truth was that I felt like the Lord had used my father to start and build CMA, but my calling was to pastor a church. I suppose, in retrospect, that even though I was closer to Dad than I had ever been, I still didn't want to live in his shadow. Like sons everywhere, I wanted to be my own man.

It was also true that Diane was very much in her element as a preacher's wife. She was an excellent leader and teacher . . . and it made me very proud to see the way the people loved her . . . and especially the women. She taught classes and seminars on Christian living for women, and they were always packed. In fact, women would come from just about every other church in town to hear her speak. Her classes were so popular that she published some of her lessons in book form.

Yes, . . . CMA was a great organization, but Diane and I were where we were supposed to be. Still, there were times when the connection to CMA was inexplicably strong.

For example, one Sunday morning a woman cornered me after our worship service and said she wanted to talk to me. I could tell that she'd been crying, so I invited her to come back into my office for a few minutes. I'd never seen her before, but she told me that she had heard that we were one church that really believed in miracles, and she needed a miracle.

I offered her a chair, sat down behind my desk and said, "What is it that you need?"

"It's my son."

I nodded. If there was anything I knew about it was rebellious sons. Maybe that was why the Lord seemed to bring so many people across my path who needed help in this area of their lives.

She rummaged around in her purse until she found an old handkerchief, and then started dabbing at her eyes.

"Go on," I said, as gently as possible. "Tell me about your son."

"Well . . . up until about a year ago, he managed a hardware store here in town. He had a lovely wife . . . and a beautiful daughter."

She was dabbing at her eyes again, and I had to wait for her to regain her composure.

"And then?" I asked.

"And then, one morning he took his wife to work. He dropped off his daughter—my granddaughter—at school, just like he always did. But instead of going to his store, he went to the bank and took all of the money out of their account. And we haven't seen him since."

"Do you have any idea where he went?"

"No, I haven't heard from him at all. Nobody has. Apparently there were financial problems. I don't know what all . . . . Pastor Shreve, I just want to hear from my son!"

"I know you do," I said. "I tell you what . . . why don't we pray about that right now."

Both of us knelt down, and we prayed that she would hear something within the next few days.

Neither one of us could have had any way of knowing that her son was hiding out in the mountains of Colorado.

Nor did we know that Dad was also in Colorado, holding an early morning service at a motorcycle rally.

The young man was in despair. He wanted to come home. But he was ashamed of what he had done. And he was afraid.

But that morning, as he was walking through the woods near the cabin where he was staying, he saw some motorcycles parked in a small clearing and decided to walk over and see what was going on.

At first, he didn't plan on getting too close. But he was touched by what he was hearing, and he wanted to hear more. By the time Dad finished his 10-minute talk, the young man went forward to ask for prayer.

That very night, he called his mother and told her that he desperately wanted to come home. He called her because he was ashamed to talk to his wife. He was home a few days later, and one of the men in the church had the privilege of leading him to the Lord.

Later on, when we pieced the sequence of events together, we determined that this young man had been in the process of praying with my dad at the very same time his mother was in my office praying with me.

As it turned out, the man's wife was not able to forgive him for what he had done, and they were soon divorced. But he re-established his relationship with his parents and his daughter, and became a shining example of God's grace and ability to change people.

Something else happened about this time that caused me to think seriously about returning to Hatfield. My folks had a terrible accident, and my mother was seriously injured.

I was on the road, conducting an evangelical crusade, when I got the news that my mother had been injured. I got the call on a Friday night following the last of a week's services, and immediately drove the 100 miles to see her.

RIDING THE CROSSROADS

I found her lying on the sofa in the living room, looking like she'd just been through ten rounds with Muhammad Ali.

Her right leg was in a cast all the way up to her hip. She was wearing a neck brace. Her head was bandaged. And what I could see of her face was bruised and swollen.

Dad was nowhere around. He was already back on the road, having ridden off for another speaking engagement. He had only been home long enough to get my mother settled as comfortably as possible.

For an instant, I felt that old anger starting to burn in me. Wasn't my mother important to him? How could he go off and leave her like this?

But, of course, I already knew the answer. Of course she was important. But as far as he was concerned, his first allegiance was always to Christ, no matter what else might happen to distract him. And there wasn't much of anything that could prevent him from being out there on the road preaching the Gospel.

It wasn't easy for Mom to talk—especially with a badly broken cheekbone. But she managed to piece together for me what had happened. She and Dad had been on the road for several weeks and she had been sick with something like pneumonia the whole time. They were on their way home when it happened.

All the way through this little town in eastern Oklahoma, they had been behind a car that was traveling about fifteen miles an hour, and they were both getting impatient. The woman driving was apparently distracted by her children, resulting in her car wandering all over the road.

Finally, just as they got to the other end of town, Dad saw his chance to go around her. He turned into the left-hand lane and gunned his motorcycle into high gear. And that's when the woman made a left-hand turn right in front of them.

They hit her broadside.

Dad was badly bruised, but Mom's injuries were far worse. Doctors patched her up as well as they could and sent her on home. I can't tell you how much it hurt me to see the way she looked. It made me regret that Diane and I lived so far away.

To explain how bad she was, a month or so later, when Mom was hobbling around on crutches, Kelly hurt himself in a motorcycle accident and had to be taken to the emergency room for some stitches. At the time, Mom still looked pretty much like "death warmed over." When she hobbled into the emergency room with Kelly, one of the nurses rushed over and extended her hand. "Ma'am," she said. "Do you need a wheelchair?"

"No," she said, gesturing at Kelly with one of her crutches. "I'm not the one who's hurt. He is!"

That was something we laughed about for years.

As badly as she was injured, that was not the end of Mom's traveling for CMA. Although it wasn't easy for her, she was soon able to get back on a motorcycle and go back out on the road again. With Mom recovered, and she and Dad traveling together again, it seemed that all was once again right with my world.

But I was about to suffer a terrible crash of my own. It was a crash that had nothing at all to do with motorcycles. And it was a crash that almost destroyed me.

CHAPTER 11

Darkness Descending

Our years in New Braunfels were wonderful for Diane and me, except for one thing. I was working at the same fevered pitch that had carried me through college. I was working so hard to bring people into God's kingdom that I didn't have any time to spend with Him myself. I waved at Him once in awhile, but that was about it. I didn't have much time for my family either. It was rare when I got to spend an evening at home with Diane and the boys. I was running much too hard and too fast, and I was on the verge of self-destruction.

A lot of what I was doing was being done in my own power. And the flesh can do a work, but it can't maintain it. The fact that I was trying to do it all by myself brought about a deep depression and fear of failure, with the result that I was burning out. Sometimes I'd lock the door to my office and sit behind my desk crying, or just staring at the wall. Nobody knew what I was going through except Diane, my secretary and my assistant pastor.

I tried to hide my desperation from my friends and family, but those three could all see through me—especially Diane. And she was worried sick about me.

And then one day I got a visit from Dottie Duke, wife of a former astronaut named Charles Duke, who knew Diane through a local Bible study. I wasn't crazy about the Dukes because they were charismatics, and I believed what I had been taught in school, that speaking in tongues was of the devil. I didn't want to have anything to do with that kind of nonsense, and so, naturally, I didn't want to have anything to do with them.

To say I was anti-charismatic would be putting it very mildly. One time, in fact, I was invited to come hold a series of services at a Baptist church which had almost been "taken over" by the charismatics. For three nights in a row, I "explained" the Bible's teaching on charismatic gifts— showing with passion, and conviction, and as many proof-texts as I could muster, that supernatural spiritual gifts were not for today, and that anyone who thought otherwise was being fooled by the devil. After my time there, that entire church repented and turned away from its errors.

In our church in New Braunfels, if anyone so much as lifted his hands during the worship service, we would ask him to leave. We wouldn't tolerate even the appearance of anything that might be construed as charismatic activity.

And in the Dukes' case it was even worse. Besides being charismatics, they were also Episcopalians, and I didn't have much use for "high church" people like that. I wasn't even sure they were Christians. After all, they sprinkled infants and called it baptism, and I thought that was ridiculous.

If Mrs. Duke had called and asked if she could come talk to me, I would have told her no thanks, that I really didn't need to hear anything she might have to say. But she didn't call. Instead, she just showed up at my office one day, demanding to see me.

When my secretary told her I was too busy to talk to anyone, Mrs. Duke said, "Lisa, I didn't call you for an appointment because I knew you wouldn't give me one!"

Then she pushed her way right past Lisa's desk and into my office, waving that Living Bible of hers in my face. (That

was another thing I didn't like about her. She read The Living Bible, which I felt was really no Bible at all.) Then she said, "God has given me a Word for you."
I tried to interrupt, but she was on a roll.

"He wants you to know that you have done a work in the flesh, but His Spirit is going to get hold of you, and you're going to do a greater work in the power of His Spirit than you ever dreamed of doing in the flesh."

Well, I was angry about her coming into my office and lecturing me in the name of God, and I didn't make any attempt to hide it. That night, I angrily told Diane about the incident and said that I wasn't about to have any "charismatic Episcopalian casting spells on me."

Diane sat thinking for awhile, then sighed and said, "Well, I wish you had *someone* you could talk to."

"I'm all right," I said.

"No! You're not all right. You're far from all right."

Diane was right. I was far from all right. And over the next few weeks, it just got worse and worse. It was like my stomach and chest were wrapped tightly in bandages and somebody was pulling them tighter . . . and . . . tighter . . . and tighter.

And then one afternoon, it all started to unravel. I knew I was falling apart, and I remembered Diane's words, "I wish you had someone you could talk to."

My thoughts turned to a man named Phil, who pastored a charismatic church in San Antonio. He was someone I would often see at Christian school conferences and other meetings. He was a charismatic, just like the Dukes, but in spite of my attempts to keep it from happening, I had grown to like him. I liked him even though I thought he was a terrible liar.

One time when I ran into him, he had just returned from India, and he started telling me about all the miracles he had seen there. As far as I was concerned, there were only two possible explanations: he was either a liar, or he was crazy.

But the truth was that right now I was in desperate need of help. It was a Wednesday evening, and I was supposed to be getting ready to conduct our church's midweek prayer service . . . but I couldn't handle it. Diane had to call my assistant and tell him he would have to cover for me. Then she called Phil and asked if we could come see him. Now, you know a Baptist preacher has really hit the bottom if he's willing to go and ask a charismatic to pray for him on a Wednesday night . . . and that's what I had done—hit the bottom!

Phil and his assistant met us at their church and took us back into their office, where they prayed fervently that God would set me free.

Nothing happened.

They were terribly disappointed, and so was I.

When they had finished, Phil's assistant told me that he owned a cabin up in the hill country and that Diane and I should go up there for a little while, just to be alone together with the Lord.

Because I was so terribly disappointed that God hadn't done something in me, I was honestly thinking about taking Diane home and then going out and driving off the first bridge I came to.

But even though that thought held a great attraction to me, I fought it off. Diane and I drove up to spend three days in fasting and prayer for God to reveal His will to us, and help me find a way out of the terrible state I was in.

Nothing happened on the first two days, and very little happened for most of the third. I was still terribly depressed and overwhelmed with fear. And then, near the end of our stay, I happened to be reading from the book of Acts. And almost immediately, something jumped out at me.

Acts 2:38-39 says, "Peter replied, 'Repent and be baptized, every one of you, in the name of Jesus Christ for the forgiveness of your sins. And you will receive the gift of the Holy Spirit. The promise is for you and your children, and for all who are far off—for all whom the Lord our God will call.'"

I felt shocked. Had those words been there all along? I had always believed that the promise of the Holy Spirit, accompanied by signs and wonders, was given only to the Christians of the first century—to one generation. But that wasn't what it said. The promise was first of all "to you," and then "to your children," and finally, "to all who are far off." The scope of that was so great. It included everyone. It included me!

I realized immediately that all of my preaching against the Holy Spirit and spiritual gifts had been wrong.

"Diane!" I shouted. "Come here for a minute! I want to show you something!"

"What? What is it?"

"Listen to this!" I read her the verse and told her about my exciting discovery.

Diane just looked at me for a moment, and then I noticed that her eyes were filling with tears.

"Diane, what's wrong? What is it?"

Between sobs she told me that she had reached the same conclusion several months earlier, but had been afraid to tell me. She was afraid that I might divorce her if I found out what she had come to believe. Her tears were tears of joy, and even though I can't explain it, something had already begun to happen in me. I could feel the depression lifting and an excitement building.

I couldn't wait to get back to San Antonio to tell Phil what

I had discovered. I was so excited that I wanted to go "right now," so that's what we did.

As soon as Phil saw me, he said, "What's happened! You look so . . . different!"

"What's happened," I said, "is that I want you to pray for me to receive the baptism . . . the filling with the Holy Spirit."

To my surprise he said no. "You want it, but you're not ready. If I pray for you to receive it and you don't, then you'll never believe it again."

I said, "If you don't show me how to receive this, I'm going to knock on every door in San Antonio until I find someone who will."

When he saw my determination, he changed his mind and agreed that he would pray for me. When he did, something like warm waves of water began washing over me and even, it seemed, through me. But then, suddenly, something awful happened. All of a sudden, I was paralyzed from the chest up, and I could not see.

Phil knew at that instant that there was a battle going on inside me. There were things inside my soul—terrible things—that kept me from surrendering fully to the Spirit of God. He and his assistant began ministering deliverance to me—casting out of me spirits of hatred, of hostility, of bitterness, fear of failure—which was something that had plagued me all my life.

I had never even heard of deliverance. I didn't know what was going on, but I could tell that wonderful changes were taking place in me. My vision came back, I was able to move freely, and I felt so exhilarated—it was like a rush of adrenalin, only much more intense. I had such joy! God was so real and so close. I felt like I could reach out and touch His face. The last vestiges of bitterness toward my dad were swept away in the torrent of God's love that washed through my being.

One of the interesting things I discovered shortly afterwards was that I was no longer afraid of the dark. I tried to play a tough guy who wasn't afraid of much of anything, but I had always been afraid of the dark. Now, that fear was completely gone. How could I be afraid of anything when the love of God surrounded me the way it did?

What had happened to me was truly terrific, but, at the same time, the last thing I was going to do was go back to my church and tell everyone about it. I saw no reason to stir up trouble in the church, so I tried to keep it between me and God.

Still, that wouldn't be easy, because I was so happy and excited. I had rediscovered the same joy I had experienced back in college when I had first discovered the truths of the Bible for myself. For so long, I had been trying to work *for* God. Now I was experiencing what it meant to have Him work *through me.*

In other words, I had always wanted to see the works of Jesus, but I had been trying to do them for Him. Now I could see that He was doing them. It was as if I was going back to John 14:12, to the place of my commitment to Jesus, and finally finding what that passage of scripture *really* meant.

I knew beyond any doubt that the Holy Spirit was at work in my life, giving me a boldness I had never had before, giving me the grace to do whatever was needed for Jesus to meet people's needs, and giving me an evangelistic fervor, with results that I had never experienced before.

For the next two weeks, a steady stream of people came to me with different prayer requests. It seemed that all of a sudden, almost every member of the congregation had a special need for prayer. And this time, I prayed for them in a new way—with power and authority—and they all knew that something had happened to me. Some of the ones who came to me were sick and in pain. The old Herbie would have prayed for God to give them strength to endure what they were going through. The new Herbie prayed passionately for healing. And guess what? Every one of them was miraculously and instantaneously healed!

It was at this time that something that had always puzzled me began to come clear. When you read the New Testament you'll find that after Jesus healed someone, He often told that person not to tell anyone what had happened. I had never really understood why Jesus had done that. But now I knew. If these people told what had happened, I would be in immediate trouble. Jesus knew that He would eventually face rejection and execution, but He had much in the way of teaching and preaching to do first, and He was taking care not to see His ministry cut short. And for the same reason, I told every one of the people I prayed for not to tell anyone else what had happened.

But one person who had been healed was so excited that she couldn't keep it to herself. She told someone who told someone else . . . and within 24 hours a special congregational meeting was called to discuss our descent into "apostasy."

The day of the night the meeting was scheduled, the man who was going to serve as the moderator came to see us. He was a man Diane and I both loved deeply—one of the original five who had helped us start the church. He had stood with us through years of hard work and growth.

He sat in our living room, fighting back tears.

"I hope you both know how much I love you," he said. "But, I disagree with you. I fear you've both lost your minds. And tonight, I'm going to have to moderate the meeting."

I nodded, "I understand. You have to do what you have to do."

But I didn't really understand. How could I? What hurt the most was that Diane and I had led most of the church members to the Lord, either directly or indirectly, and now they were going to ask us to leave. They were following what I had taught them. But it hurt so bad to be rejected like that. It took me back to another time, when, as a boy of twelve, I had sat in a meeting and heard my father verbally torn apart. I didn't want to go through that again. Diane and I both knew that the outcome of the meeting was already decided anyway, so we decided that we wouldn't even go.

When our friend asked me if I wanted him to say anything on our behalf, I asked him to say that we were being relieved of our duties with the church because we believed what the Bible said in Mark 16:15-20. Then I asked him if he would please read that scripture to those in attendance. He did exactly as I asked, and when he finished reading that passage from Mark, several people got up and walked out of the meeting. They knew then that we were being fired because we believed everything the Bible said, and they wanted no part of it.

It was after 10:00 p.m. when the phone call came informing us that I had been fired effective immediately. The vote had been nearly unanimous. I have to admit that even though we knew it was coming, and even though God's presence was especially strong that night, Diane and I both wept when we got the news.

In addition to the wonderful presence of God, one of the things that got me through the next few weeks was my relationship with CMA. In the preceding few months I had become more involved with the organization. As CMA's growth continued to be spectacular, I had been called upon more frequently to conduct evangelism seminars and other CMA-related meetings. Dad had put together a wonderful group of people to run CMA and I loved them. Besides that, Dad had never given up on the idea that someday I would come to work for CMA full-time.

It wasn't something he brought up all the time. I certainly didn't feel any pressure from him. But every once in awhile, he let me know that he would love to see me come on board. But it still wasn't what I wanted to do—even at this time when I didn't know what my next move ought to be.

But instead of accepting Dad's offer, Diane and I took a few weeks to seek the Lord's direction to see where we ought to go from here.

Finally, it seemed clear that God was telling us to start another church. So that's what we did.

Those were exciting days, but also a bit confusing, since I was going through a complete restructuring of my "theology." That little church began to grow, not only in numbers, but in the power of God.

Our people were taking the power of God out into the community. They were taking God with them to work and school—into the office, the factory, the classroom, looking for opportunities to pray with friends, co-workers and fellow students whenever and wherever possible. As a result, people were healed, delivered, had their emotional and physical needs met, and *then* it was easy to lead them to Christ. Many people were saved, and we grew from a handful of people to as many as 200 on a Sunday morning.

But it was a temporary learning time. Diane and I both felt that. God had something else planned for us. The strangest part of it was that in the midst of God's blessing,

I felt that something was missing. Every time I traveled for CMA, I seemed drawn more and more to evangelism. But even then, I resisted the idea of going on the road full-time because I remembered how much I had resented Dad's frequent trips when I was a boy. And yet, as I talked to the CMA evangelists—as I heard their wonderful stories about the way the Spirit of God was moving "out there,"—I felt a very strong pull to join them. Yes, we were reaching the lost here in New Braunfels . . . but the Father heart of God wanted more from me.

He seemed to be telling me that I had something special to offer. I knew what it meant to live in rebellion. I knew what it meant to feel rejected, scorned and unloved. I knew how it felt to think that there wasn't anyone anywhere who loved you. And then, I knew what it was like to rediscover a father's love.

God seemed to be saying to me, "There are so many like that out there, Herbie. So many who feel the way you used to feel. They need to know My love."

It was while I was thinking about all of these things that Roy Johnson, who, by this time, was serving as one of CMA's directors, talked to me.

"Herbie," he said, "why don't you come to work full-time for CMA?" I told him that Diane and I would pray about it. In the process of praying about it, we traveled to Hatfield on my motorcycle and discussed with Dad what was on both of our hearts.

Later, as we talked about things over a cup of coffee, Diane said, "Herbie, you know the Lord is doing this."

"Yes, I know," I sighed. "But I don't want to raise my kids via the telephone.

"But you can't fight what the Lord is doing."

Right again, Diane.

And so, before we headed back for Texas, we knew I would accept their offer to come on board as director of teaching and training.

Then we went back home and tried to tell the members of our church.

And we couldn't do it. Well, actually, I'm the one who couldn't do it. For eight weeks, I tried and failed. That's how much I loved those people, and how much I feared hurting them.

Three times we had the church leaders over for dinner. Three times they stayed until midnight. Three times I tried to tell them that the reason we had invited them over was so that I could tell them I was leaving, but couldn't find the words.

More than three times I told Diane, "This is it. This coming Sunday, I'm going to announce from the pulpit that we have decided to go back to Arkansas to go to work for CMA." But when I stood in the pulpit looking out at all those beautiful faces, faces of people who loved God so much, and who loved us, too, I couldn't do that either. Finally, though, I realized there was no way around it. If I wanted to take the full-time job with CMA, I was going to have to get on with it.

And so, choking back tears, I made the announcement from the pulpit on a Sunday morning.

The response was pretty much what I expected. Lots of tears. Lots of people asking us if we were sure that this was what God wanted for us. Quite a few people told us that they knew we had missed God on this.

But we knew better. We knew that he was opening the door to an exciting new adventure. And so, Diane and I packed up the kids—four of them by this time, including Benji and one-year-old Misty, both of whom had been born in New Braunfels—and headed back to Hatfield. We were going home.

We knew that it would be the beginning of a new and exciting adventure.

But we didn't know the half of it.

CHAPTER 12

Dear God, Why Does
It Have to Hurt So Much?

I'd like to tell you that Diane and I took the kids back to
Hatfield and that we all lived happily ever after, riding bikes
and witnessing for the Christian Motorcyclists Association.

Sorry. This is real life.

Sometimes things weren't so great. Sometimes they were
downright awful. But in the worst of it, we both knew that
we were exactly where God wanted us to be.

By this time, CMA had more than 200 chapters all over
the United States, with more than 20,000 members, and so
Dad and I were on the road almost constantly that first year.
We rarely saw each other.

I would leave home with only a few dollars in my pocket,
not knowing how I was going to make it past the first few
days on the road, and even though God always provided,
there were many times when we barely squeaked by.

In a lot of ways, history was repeating itself. Diane and I
were learning for ourselves how God would take care of us,
the same way Mom and Dad had learned the lesson some
years before.

For example, I remember one time when Diane came
with me to the post office just before I was preparing to
leave home for four weeks. We were hoping there would
be some money there. We stayed alive during those years
through the occasional gifts that came in the mail from peo-

ple who appreciated our ministry. That day, sure enough, there was some money in our post office box. Around $60. Diane and I both agreed that I needed to take the money and go, so that's what I did.

I prayed that the Lord would provide for us the way He had always provided for my folks. And He did. Somehow, we both survived that time. We never missed any payments for rent or bills, and the kids never went hungry.

There was one major difference, though, between what I was going through and what Dad had gone through. That was that when he had started out, he, Mom and Kelly had taken a great deal of abuse because of their stand for Jesus. They were ridiculed, harassed, mocked, and threatened, and they never backed down. They kept on loving people who tried their very best to be unlovable. And eventually they won them over. They came to be honored, rather than ridiculed, for their stand for Jesus, even by those who demonstrated by their actions that they wanted nothing to do with the Christian lifestyle.

In other words, they paved the way for people like me. I'm not saying there weren't times when I was put down or mocked because I was with CMA—certainly there were— but things were not nearly as bad for me as they had been for my parents. It was thanks, in large part, to people like them that CMA gained the respect it has today.

Still, it wasn't easy going out on the road knowing that I was leaving Diane home without any extra money for emergencies that might arise. For even though I was now in a full-time position with CMA, I did not have a full-time salary. At that time, CMA required everyone who joined the staff to ride for at least a year without financial support. That was an excellent way of finding out if God really wanted someone to be involved in CMA on a full-time basis. It also helped to weed out those who weren't really committed to CMA's goals and purposes. We had many more applicants than we had positions available, and we wanted people to be able to cover their own expenses. That applied to everybody, no matter what position you might be filling.

We even had a rule—and still do—that you were not allowed to let your needs be known while you were out on the road. If we heard of instances where one of our evangelists had said something like, "Pray for me because I need a new set of tires," we would call him in and tell him forcefully not to do that sort of thing anymore. And if such behavior continued, that person would be dismissed. We were not about to let anyone manipulate people into giving him things. For the sake of our ministry, we were determined to maintain the organization's integrity at all costs.

If you had a real need, you were to let the CMA staff, your church family or your immediate family know, and that was it. If your need couldn't be met from those three sources, we expected that God would meet it some other way. We also expected that God would take care of our families while we were on the road. But, like I said, it wasn't always easy to hold onto that kind of faith. My major worry was the expense of traveling so many miles on an older bike that guzzled gas and was often in need of repair. Sometimes I wondered how I was going to make it from one rally to the next. But God always provided.

That was an especially tough time for Diane, because she had left all of her friends behind in Texas. Not only that, but she had been an integral part of the ministry there, and now I was off traveling while she stayed home.

We lived in an old farmhouse that was out in the country, separated by a somewhat rickety bridge from the main highway. And even though this was home to Diane and her family lived nearby, she had been away for ten years. She had become accustomed to life in the city and had to learn all over again how to live in a rural area. Diane was often lonely and frustrated, and it was easy to see why.

For her, all that loneliness and frustration came to an explosion during two disastrous days early in 1985.

The day before I was to leave on a long trip, I borrowed a chain saw from my grandfather because I wanted to cut some firewood to sell. Unfortunately, I bent over at one point and my glasses fell off, right into the teeth of the saw. Before I could even think about rescuing them, they were torn to shreds.

They were my only pair so I had to head out on the road without them.

Then, the first day I was gone, an electrical storm hit our antenna and blew out the picture tube on our television set. As if that weren't enough, Diane put a big load of laundry in the washing machine, only to have the thing give up the ghost halfway through, leaving the clothes soaking in soapy water. And then, as she was dealing with that emergency, the telephone rang. It was the landlord calling to tell us that he had just sold the house out from under us. We had to vacate within thirty days.

All of that in the space of twenty-four hours would have been enough to drive the strongest person to her knees. But there was more.

The kids were acting up. Well, they weren't acting up so much as they were just being kids—fussing and fighting in the "Mom, he touched me," "He touched me first," way that kids have been fussing and fighting since the days of Cain and Abel.

But on top of everything else, and without me there to help her referee, Diane just couldn't take it anymore. She stormed out of the house, not really knowing where she was headed, walked halfway across a field, where she stopped and "had it out" with God.

"Father," she shouted at the sky, "I don't know how much of this I can take! We've been trusting You to take care of us, but just look what's happened!"

She went on to tell Him about the situation with the house, the problem with the washing machine, the television set, my glasses, and so on. She understood that she wasn't telling Him anything He didn't already know, but she felt like she needed to recount it all for Him just the same.

She talked to the Lord that way for a good half hour, just unburdening her heart, not in anger so much as in confusion and frustration.

"Lord," she cried, "I hope You're not angry with me for talking to You this way, but I've got to let You know how I feel."

As she kept talking, she was suddenly very aware of the fact that God was listening to her. She understood now what the Psalmist David was doing throughout the Psalms as he poured out his heart to God. Oh, she always knew that God was listening when she prayed, but this time there was a real sense that He was listening with a deep concern and understanding. And He was giving her His reassurance that yes, He did care. He would be with us. She felt the calm strength of His presence pouring into her soul.

Diane later told me that she couldn't really explain what had happened. There hadn't been any great revelation. No flash of light. No burning bush. Not even an audible voice. Nothing, in fact, but the sound of the wind passing through the grass. But somehow, she had experienced a complete emotional healing at that moment, and she went back into the house refreshed and ready to carry on.

She realized, that day, that I wasn't the only one who had

a ministry. *Everyone* has a ministry of some sort. At present, her ministry would be to the women of our community. And so she started a Bible study in our home. That Bible study continued for several years, and it became a great influence for Christ in the Mena/Hatfield area. Just as they had done in New Braunfels, women came from almost every church in town to listen to Diane teach from the Bible. Those women loved the Lord, and they grew to love each other. Most of Diane's very best friendships eventually grew out of that Bible study group.

Right away, the Lord cemented the bond between those women by means of a vicious electrical storm that nearly blew the house down. There were 18 people gathered in our house that evening, including mothers and children. And, at the end of their time together, just as they were starting to clean up, the worst storm of the year came up out of nowhere. Suddenly, there was a brilliant flash of light, followed immediately by a crashing boom of thunder. That lightning was just outside the door! Quickly, the wind began to howl and the rain started to fall so fast it sounded like a waterfall splashing onto the roof.

Diane knew that tornadoes were frequent visitors to this part of the country so she took one of the women aside and said, "Do you think maybe we should go into the hall?"

Looking around at the large windows in the living room, Diane's friend nodded her head. "That's a good idea."

"Everyone! Everyone!" Diane shouted. "I think we'd all better move into the hall . . . just in case?"

Quickly, the women gathered up babies, purses, Bibles— whatever they could grab—and crowded into the hall just off the living room. There were women from almost every church in town in that hall—Assembly of God, Baptist, Methodist, Church of Christ—some who had been walking with the Lord for years, and others who were very new in the faith. As the storm heightened, these women all began to pray in the ways they felt most comfortable. After it was over, no one was offended at the style of prayer any of the women chose. Those things don't matter in the least when you're praying for your children's lives.

Almost immediately after they gathered in the hallway, there was a loud crash followed by the tinkling sound of glass. A window had been blown out, and bits of glass had showered the area where they had been seated only moments before. Had they still been in there, someone definitely would have been injured by the flying glass. Then everything went dark. Power lines were down.

The storm was so violent that it toppled several trees on our property, some of them big oaks that had been standing for fifty years or more. Some of them fell across the only road that connected our house to the main highway, and it took hours for their worried husbands to cut the trees and clear the road.

Thankfully, nobody was hurt. And the time the women spent sitting in the dark together, praying, and holding on to each other built a tremendous bond between them. By the time they left our house that night, a true sisterly bond had developed between those women.

While Diane was ministering to the women of our community, I was spending so much time on the road that I sometimes didn't even know for sure where I was. When you're on the Interstate, it's hard to tell even what state you're in, because so much of the scenery looks the same.

About this time, a young man named Victor Rowell became involved with CMA, and Dad asked if I would ride with him.

I didn't want to. Victor was all right, but he was just a kid, and I didn't want any kid slowing me down. I had known Victor for years, ever since he was a pre-schooler, and now he had just graduated from high school and was preparing to go to college. In fact, the church he attended had said they would pay for his college education if he would come back after graduation and spend some time serving as their youth minister. And there was no doubt in my mind that Victor would make a great youth minister.

But his father had a different idea.

"If you really want to learn what ministering to others is all about," his dad had told him, "why don't you get out there and ride with CMA?"

Victor had known all about CMA from its very beginning. In fact, he had been playing under the table with Kelly when Dad first brought a group of men together at our house to discuss the idea of starting a ministry to motorcyclists. As for my part, I liked Victor and I had always admired the close, loving relationship he had with his father. Victor had accepted Christ at a very early age and he had never wavered. And I admired that, too.

I should have known that if God wanted Victor to ride along with me, there wasn't anything I could do to stop it. But all I saw was that I didn't want him tagging along with me, and I told my dad so in the bluntest possible terms.

"Oh, come on, I know Victor. He'll do great."

Yeah. My dad knew Victor all right. He had always thought he knew me, too, even when I was sneaking off to smoke pot every day at the end of our ride together.

But Dad wouldn't let me refuse.

"Okay," I finally agreed. "But I'm not going to slow down and wait for him. If he wants to go with me, he'd better keep up."

Dad shrugged. "Fine. Tell him how you feel."

That's exactly what I did. Before our first trip together I sat him down.

"Listen, Victor," I said. "I want you to know that you're

free to make your own decisions out there. If I pull over to get a hamburger and you want a steak, get a steak. If I get a steak and you want a hamburger, fine. If I keep going but you want to stop, go ahead and stop."

Victor just nodded and smiled. He understood.

We would see about that.

Our first day together, I rode something like 600 miles. He stayed with me every inch of the way and never even talked about stopping. Over the next few weeks we rode some unbelievable hours, and Victor never flinched. Mile after mile, hour after hour, my admiration grew for the guy. He was a trooper, no doubt about it.

I quickly changed my mind about him and was happy to have him along. When we came back into town for a few days, he would head over to his job at the grocery store, where he'd put in as many hours as possible before we headed out of town again. It got to the point where I wondered how *he* did it. And to think, I was afraid he was going to slow *me* down!

Sometimes, I was so desperate to see my family that I rode unbelievably long hours, and Victor stayed right with me. For example, I'd ride from California to Arkansas just so I could see Diane and the kids, only to turn around the next day and head back to Arizona for a rally. I rode so much that all night long in my dreams I saw the broken white line of the interstate flashing in front of me! I would've felt better if Victor had shown *some* signs of exhaustion but he didn't.

We rode together for two years, and it was causing us grief because we didn't have a full-time role for him within the organization.

Then one day, Victor came in and started telling me about a dream he had. I was on my motorcycle headed down the highway in one direction, and he was going the other way. He could see that his motorcycle had a word painted on it, but he didn't know what the word meant.

I wasn't familiar with the word either, but suggested that he might try to look it up. Later that day, he went to the library, where he discovered that the word in his dream is a Hebrew word that means "fully equipped warrior." When he came back and told me what he had discovered, I knew immediately that God had special plans for Victor, and I was sure that, somehow, those plans would involve CMA. Victor had no knowledge of Hebrew. He couldn't have made that word up, and I knew God's hand was upon him.

However, it was still some time before we were able to open a full-time position for him. He even stayed home for awhile and put together his own business. But as soon as we were able to do it, we brought him on board as our youth director, and he has done an incredible job of bringing teenagers and young adults to the Lord.

Watching Victor was good for me in a lot of ways, but one of the most important was that it gave me the hope that my own kids didn't have to go through the same period of rebellion and disillusionment that had held me captive for so many years.

Because I was determined that I wouldn't let the same sort of resentment develop in my children that I had felt toward my father, I asked different friends and family members to keep an eye on their countenances. If they saw any lingering sadness or anger, if their faces began to show weariness or their shoulders began to droop, I wanted to know about it. That would be a sign that I was spending too much time on the road, and I would do what I could to change the situation.

I also took the kids with me whenever it was possible.

For example, on one occasion I had been home less than an hour after returning from a three-week trip to California when the phone rang. It was one of our evangelists, a man who was supposed to speak at a rally in Pennsylvania the day after tomorrow. Unfortunately, he had a family emergency and could not make the trip. Because it was a big rally, we needed to have a presence there, and I was the only one available.

What's more, if I was going to get there on time, I had to leave almost immediately. I wasn't happy about it. I wanted to spend some time with my family! And so, on the impulse of the moment, I decided that I would hook up the sidecar and take the two older boys, Jeff and Randy, with me.

I don't know how old they were at the time—probably no more than seven and five. Diane agreed they needed to be with me, despite the fact that I had virtually no money to take with me in case of any emergencies that might arise.

The first night we rode all the way from Hatfield to Memphis, where we slept on a table at a roadside park. I know that must sound crazy, but we didn't have money to do anything else. Then, the next day, we drove straight from Memphis all the way to Pennsylvania.

Just before we got to the rally I was almost entirely out of cash. The boys hadn't eaten anything since a small bite that morning and I knew they were hungry. *My* stomach was growling, and I knew that, as little as they were, they must be feeling it worse than I was.

"Listen, boys," I said, "when we get to the rally, I'll be able to get us something to eat. But right now, I don't have enough money. If I bought us something to eat, I wouldn't have any money left for gas. Maybe I can get us some crackers or something, but we'll have to wait until after the service tonight before we can have anything else."

Even though the boys were so small, they understood. They didn't complain. If I had to spend the money on gas, that was just the way it was, and they'd wait patiently until I had some money for food. Of course, what they didn't realize was that I was speaking "in faith" about being able to get something to eat after that night's rally. Other than that, there was no guarantee.

So we stopped for gas, and when I came out of the cashier's office, I saw that another customer had gone over and was talking to the boys. When I walked up he said, "I was just telling your boys here how much I like your sidecar."

"Thank you."

"Your boys tell me you've come all the way from Arkansas."

"That's right. We're on our way to a motorcycle rally."

"Well, I think that's just great. Good to see a family traveling together like this."

Then he wished us well, got into his car, and drove off down the street.

After watching him go, I told the boys that after paying for the gasoline, I still had enough money left for one packet of toasted cheese and peanut butter crackers. There were six crackers in the pack, so that meant we would each get two of them. That would have to be enough for now. We divvied up the crackers, and then we all got ready to get back on the road.

But just as we were pulling out of the gas station, I heard a horn honking, and looked up to see the same man we had been talking to earlier. He had driven down the street, made a U-turn, and was coming back, honking and waving at me to stay where I was.

He pulled up beside me, jumped out of his car and ran over.

"Listen," he said, "I don't normally do anything like this, and I hope you're not insulted. But I think it's so neat that you've got your boys out here and everything. And . . . if

143

you don't mind . . . I'd like to give you twenty dollars so you can have some fun together on me."

"Well, are you sure . . ."

"Sure, I'm sure. I just think this is great!"

So did we. We thanked the man, and stopped at the next fast-food place we saw, where we filled our aching stomachs with hamburgers and fries.

My boys were excited about seeing the way God had provided for us, and so was I. As it turned out, we got to the rally ten minutes before I was scheduled to speak, and this after riding straight through for nearly 24 hours. How could there be any doubt that God was with us?

There were other trips like that, but the sad thing for me was that I couldn't take the kids with me as often as I wanted to. I couldn't just take them out of school for weeks at a time, so I usually had to leave them at home. And I continued to be afraid that they would come to resent me the way I had grown to resent my father when I was a child.

So I had a talk with them. Misty was really too young to understand much of what was going on, but I wanted the boys to know that they had the right to tell me any time that I had been gone too much. Not only the right, really, but the responsibility. I wanted to do what God wanted me to do, but I knew that my first responsibility was to Diane and the kids.

"If you think I'm gone too much, just tell me," I said. "I might not be able to fix it right away, but I'll start working on it. And I promise you, I *will* fix it."

It was Benji who took me up on my promise.

A few months later, when I was home for a couple of days, Benji, who was nearly six, asked me if I'd go with him for a walk.

He was so happy to be with me, and I returned the feeling.

RIDING THE CROSSROADS

As we walked along a country lane together, I kept looking at him, and thinking how much I loved my kids. The bond between a father and his son can be such an incredible feeling. I was smiling at the way Benji was running circles around me. Where on earth did he get so much energy? He stopped to throw rocks. He chased birds. He kicked anything kickable that happened to be in our path. Just watching him made me tired. After awhile, he seemed to be tiring, too, because he came back beside me, reached up and took my hand, and was content just to walk along with me for awhile, completely in silence.

Finally, he spoke, "Dad . . . do you remember when you told us that if you were gone too much we could tell you and that you'd fix it."

"Of course I remember that, Benji. And I meant it."

He was quiet for another moment.

"Um . . . would it be okay to tell you that now?"

"Of course it would."

"Well . . . it seems like you're never home. You come in and wash your clothes and then you leave again. And I miss you when you're gone."

I squatted down and hugged him tightly. "I'm glad you told me that, Benji. Now, you know, I can't fix it right away, but I promise, I'll start working on it."

He was so happy and so proud. He stuck out his chest as if I'd just pinned the Medal of Honor on it, and he strutted off feeling very happy and very good about himself.

That night, I told Diane about my conversation with our youngest son, and we talked well into the night about what we could do to remedy the situation. Finally, we made the decision that we would do two things. First, I would do what I could to cut back the number of days I was on the road. Second, we would start traveling together as a family as much as possible.

That was going to take some doing. If we were going to travel together, it meant that Diane was going to have to learn how to ride a motorcycle—one with a sidecar attached. Diane was more than willing to learn, but before she could do that, we'd have to get another motorcycle and another sidecar. How in the world were we going to do that? We didn't have any money, but we did have prayer, and we would just have to start praying that the Lord would provide. In the meantime, I continued to take the kids as often as possible.

Right after Benji's sixth birthday he traveled with me to a rally in East Texas. We had a family rule that you couldn't ride on the back of a motorcycle until you were six, so Benji was feeling very grown-up and proud when his time finally came.

For Christmas the previous year, I had made some leather chaps for the boys so they all looked like midget bikers, and Benji looked so cool sitting up there on a motorcycle.

Unfortunately, that first trip didn't start off too great. It rained on us off and on all the way to the rally. And it was cold. Then, when we got to the rally, I saw quickly that this was no place for a small boy. The smell of marijuana smoke hung heavy in the air, and beer was flowing freely from several kegs that had been set up around a blazing campfire.

As Benji and I joined the other rally-goers around the campfire, I was thinking, "Man, his mother would be furious if she knew what kind of a place I brought him to."

Oh, oh. Where was he? He had been here just a minute ago, but now . . . . Wait! There he is!

Benji was heading toward me, hand in hand with some huge, hairy biker. The guy looked like a mountain to begin with, and standing there next to Benji, he looked like Mount Everest! What in the world was this guy doing with my little boy? This fellow was so hairy, I couldn't even see his mouth, so I didn't know if he was smiling, or frowning, or coming to punch me in the nose because Benji was bothering him. But as they got closer, I was relieved to see a definite twinkle in his eye.

As they came up to me, Benji reached up and put his new-found friend's hand in mind. "This is my daddy! He's the one I was telling you about."

"Um . . . ." the big guy seemed embarrassed. "Hello sir. I've been talkin' to your boy."

"Good to meet you," I said.

"Now if you've got any problems," Benji went on, "I know he can help you. Well . . . see you later."

And he ran off to find someone else to talk to.

All that night, Benji kept bringing people to me, and before we went off to bed, at least three of them had given their lives to Christ. I didn't have to worry about Benji or wonder where he was, because I would keep hearing his shrill little voice.

"How long you been ridin' Harleys, Mister?"

A deep, gruff voice would answer back, "Oh . . . I've been ridin' 20, 25 years I guess."

"Well that's nothin'. I been riding 'em all my life." By the time he said that, he had their hearts.

And then, "You haven't met my daddy have you? Well, he's an evangelist with CMA and he can help you. I know you got problems. Everybody has problems. Come on, I want you to meet my daddy!"

Benji was having an absolutely wonderful time, and what's more, I thought we made a pretty terrific team. He softened their hearts for me, and made my job a lot easier!

We spent a couple of days at the rally and had a great time together before heading home late on Sunday night. We hadn't gone too far down the highway when a car behind me started honking its horn—over and over. I figured something must be wrong, so I turned into the far right-hand lane and began to slow down. Looking back over my shoulder, I saw what all the honking was about. Benji was fast asleep and was hanging backwards over the trunk.

The poor little guy was exhausted. It had been a long, hard trip for him. Although I had done my best for him, I realized that his mama would have done better. She would have made sure that he got to bed early enough to get the sleep he needed, instead of staying up half the night "witnessing" to outlaw bikers.

Yes, indeed. Something was going to have to change. And soon.

CHAPTER 13

The Family That Travels Together

"Come on Diane . . . it's no big deal. *Anyone* can do it!"
Her eyes flashed in anger at my condescending tone.
"Anyone can do it? Well, I guess I must be the most inept
person on earth then, huh?"

"Look," I said, "riding a motorcycle is just like riding a
horse. You fall off, you get back on. It's that simple."

"Oh, it is, is it?"

The expression on her face changed. Where there had
been anger a moment ago, now I saw only hurt and frustration.

"Well, I just hope I don't die trying," she said.

All of a sudden, a scene from long ago began replaying
through my mind. I saw a frightened and bruised little boy.
I saw a horse that was determined that nobody was going
to ride him. And I saw a father who was just as determined
that his son was going to ride that horse no matter what.

"Diane," I said. "I'm sorry. I know you're trying. It's just
so hard for me to be away from you all the time, and . . ."

"And it's hard for me, too," she interrupted. "But I just
can't seem to get the hang of it. Not on this big old thing."

It was a beautiful Saturday morning in late fall, and Diane
and I had been out in front of the house for hours. She was
trying to learn how to ride the very-old, very-used motorcycle I had managed to buy for her, and though I knew she
was trying hard, my patience was wearing thin. I wanted

149

Diane and the kids to start traveling with me by the time February rolled around, and on this particular morning I was having very severe doubts about that. We had so much work to do!

I had started her off the same way I had learned to ride. With the motorcycle standing on its center stand, she had climbed aboard and I had shown her how to use the clutch, run her through the gears, and so on. After a half-hour or so of that, I figured she was ready to take her first solo ride . . . but she looked a lot better with that bike on the center stand than she did speeding down the driveway at, say, about three miles per hour, wobbling as if she were trying to ride off in 57 different directions at once. That's about as fast as she'd get it going before it would fall over. Several times, the bike fell, and Diane staggered away. A couple of times she went sprawling into the dirt. But every time, I helped her pick herself up, dusted her off, and hurried her back aboard.

At first, the kids were excited about watching their mother learn how to ride a motorcycle. Then they were frightened—especially little Misty—when they saw her take so many tumbles. And finally, they gave up and went back into the house to watch Saturday morning cartoons.

"Big old thing?" Was that what Diane had said?

"You know," I told her, "I think you've hit on it."

"Hit on what?"

"The problem."

"The problem is that I'm probably going to kill myself."

"No, it's not," I laughed. "The problem is that you need a smaller motorcycle. In fact, I don't know what I was thinking in the first place."

"You really think that would make a difference?" she asked, looking hopeful for the first time all morning.

"I know it," I said. "What do you say we take this 'big old

thing' back and see if we can't find something more suitable."

That's what we did, and it helped. Diane did much better on a smaller bike. She rode around and around our property in first gear—as much as I encouraged her, she still wasn't ready to shoot for second or third gears. Unfortunately, she still had a bit of trouble trying to stop without letting the bike fall over. But we were making tremendous progress, and I was proud of her.

Our lessons continued over the next several weeks, whenever I was home, and, as time went by, the stops were coming smoother and smoother. The bike was hardly ever falling over now, and we were actually venturing out of the driveway and onto the main highway. Still ahead lay the task of learning how to ride a motorcycle with a sidecar attached. And then, too, there was also the matter of finding a sidecar, which we couldn't exactly afford. But we were confident that if our plans were in God's will, He would provide for us when the time was right.

There were still a few moments of disaster along the way.

One time when she was aggravated about letting the bike fall over, she reached down to pick it up without looking to see what she was doing and grabbed hold of the tailpipe. That resulted in burns across her palm and several fingers.

Another time, we rode our motorcycles all the way to her mother's house, a distance of several miles.

Diane told me later that she prayed for green lights all the way, and the Lord graciously answered her prayers. We didn't hit one red light, and Diane rode beautifully. Not a lick of trouble—and we had a good time telling her mother all about our plans to start traveling together as a family.

When it came time to go, I led the way, with Diane right behind me. I stopped at the end of the driveway and looked in the rear-view mirror. Diane was right behind me.

Good. I looked both ways. No traffic. Good. I pulled out, slowly turned left and proceeded down the highway. I glanced in the rear-view mirror again. No Diane. I pulled over and waited. Still no Diane. I turned around and looked behind me. Where was she?

I found her sitting in a ditch, uninjured, except for her pride. It seems that instead of turning left, she had gone straight across the highway and into the ditch.

"Are you okay?" I asked.

"Yes, I'm fine!" She shot the words at me.

"Well . . . what happened?"

"I don't know," she said. "I turned. But the bike didn't."

I tried to stop myself but I couldn't. I threw back my head and roared with laughter. Thankfully, Diane joined in. After we'd had a good laugh about it, I helped her out of the ditch, and we made it the rest of the way home without incident.

Our next step was to take a trip of about fifty miles, and Diane rode like an old pro . . . until we were on the way home. Once again, I was in the lead, keeping a careful eye on the rear-view mirror. And once again, she was there one minute and gone the next.

This time, the elements had teamed up to defeat her. First, we were heading West into the setting sun, so visibility was poor. And, second, we came to a curve in the road. Diane told me later that she knew immediately that she wasn't going to make that turn. Instead, she kept going straight, off the road and into someone's front yard, where she wound up sprawled in the grass. As she picked up her aching body, she heard a voice calling to her.

"You all right?"

She looked up to see an elderly gentleman looking over the railing of his porch. Suddenly her pride hurt much worse than the bruises and abrasions from her fall.

He called out to her again, "Are you all right, fella?"
That did it. "Fella," was more than she could take.
Ripping off her helmet so that her long hair fell onto her shoulders, she shouted, "I'm a girl! And, yes, I'm all right!"

I had to convince Diane to get back aboard the motorcycle that time, and it wasn't easy. But to her credit, she finally did it. And she made it the rest of the way home just fine.

December came and went, and although Diane was turning into a first-class motorcyclist, we still had no sidecar. No prospects of a sidecar. No money for a sidecar. But we did have prayer, and the reassurance that God's will was for us to start riding together as a family. What worried me most was that I had already divided my trips that year into eight-week segments. And when the time came for me to leave, I had to go. If we didn't have a sidecar by that time, I'd have to head out on the road by myself, and I'd have to stay gone for two months.

It was late in January, only two weeks away from our scheduled first trip together, when a woman in Texas called and told us that she had a sidecar and a motorcycle, and that she felt led to give them to us.

I thought, at first, that I had misunderstood her.

"How much do you want for them?" I asked.

"No, no. I didn't say *sell* them. I said *give* them."

"Are you sure?"

She laughed. "God told me to give them to you," she said. "And I'm not about to argue with God."

Neither were we. Once again, I was awed and humbled by the way God works everything out. He never misses a beat!

At the same time, that meant that I had two weeks to get Diane to the point where she was comfortable with a sidecar to leave on a 10,000-mile trip.

Our first lesson came the following Saturday.

I took her out to the main road, which thankfully, didn't present much of a traffic problem.

"Okay, Diane," I told her. "I'm going to get in the sidecar, while you drive. If I see that you're going too far to the left or right . . . well, you just listen to me and I'll tell you what to do."

"Are you sure that's . . . ."

"Sure I'm sure." I put my arm around her and gave her a quick kiss. "You're gonna do great!"

We started off down the road, and, at first, she *was* doing great.

"Terrific!" I yelled. "You're doing fantastic!"

"What?"

"Fantastic!" I shouted as loud as I could, and that time I knew she heard me, because she smiled, although she didn't take her eyes off the road.

As we continued on our way, Diane began to drift closer and closer to the right-hand shoulder, a dangerous move in a stretch of road lined with rural mailboxes.

"Diane, move to the left!" I yelled.

No response.

"Diane . . . you're too far to the right!"

"Left! Left!" I screamed.

Diane couldn't hear me over the roar of the motorcycle engine. She told me later that she knew I was saying something, but that she had no idea what it was. She just assumed that I was trying to give her more encouragement!

I swung my arms to show her that she needed to move left . . . but she didn't see me. Her hands were fastened to the handlebars, and her eyes were just as fastened on the road in front of her!

"Diane! Diane!"

At the very last moment, she realized what was happening, turned to the left, and just barely managed to avoid the offense of destroying government property. In other words, she managed to miss the mailbox, and I'm still not sure how, except that nothing is impossible for God. After that inauspicious start, Diane learned quickly, and we never had any more trouble. By the time of our scheduled departure date, we were ready to go. We bundled the kids in our sidecars—the oldest two, Jeff and Randy in hers, and the two little ones, Ben and Misty in mine—and headed off down the highway—amazed once again, but not surprised, by God's loving faithfulness. No matter what lay ahead, we were in His care. And there were going to be many times when we needed to remember that.

CHAPTER 14

Miracles!

The road is no place for children to grow up. No doubt about it.

But at the same time, I wouldn't take a billion dollars for the few years we spent traveling together as a family.

In a lot of ways, it wasn't easy for any of us.

Diane had her work cut out for her, trying to home school four children during the small amount of time that was available to her while we attended various motorcycle rallies throughout the country. And it certainly wasn't easy to keep everybody properly clothed, fed, and bathed, what with the irregular hours we were keeping. Also, as anybody who's ever traveled with children knows, you can't go too far without *somebody* needing to take a bathroom break or get a drink. Still, our kids developed remarkable patience and self-control, and being on the road made us one of the closest-knit families I know.

If you were to ask my kids today, what it was like being on the road all the time, who knows what they might say?

They might tell you, "Oh, it was being cold . . . being rained on . . . not having any money for food," and so on. But you'll see the twinkle in their eyes when they're telling you those things. You'll hear the laughter in their voices, and you'll know that, just like Diane and me, they wouldn't trade those experiences for anything.

One of the best things about those days was that we were all constant witnesses to the miraculous love of God.

The first year we were all on the road together, Diane and I were both riding older bikes that had seen a lot of highways and byways. In that one year, we added another 40,000 miles or so to motorcycles that had already seen enough miles to last a lifetime. My bike especially was old, ragged, and had a voracious appetite for oil and gasoline. That thing rattled and smoked and hiccupped. Sometimes the kids would have to get out of the sidecar to push it to get it started.

I had been praying for months, "Lord, if you want me to ride something better, You're going to have to give it to me. But if this doesn't embarrass You, I guess it doesn't embarrass me." Apparently it didn't embarrass Him.

We were in Southern California after being on the road for weeks and decided to take the kids to Disneyland. We didn't do that sort of thing very often because we didn't have the money. But the kids had been so good, and they deserved a treat. So we headed out on a Thursday morning in the direction of Mickey Mouse and Company. We hadn't told the kids where we were going because we wanted it to be a surprise.

We figured we'd spend the day in "The Magic Kingdom," and then we'd ride out to Hemet—some sixty miles or so to the east—where we were to take part in a rally on Friday and Saturday.

And even though I hate to admit it, Diane knew the way to Disneyland, but I didn't believe her.

We were riding side by side down the freeway, when she pointed toward an upcoming off-ramp.

I shook my head.

She pointed again.

I shook my head again, more vigorously this time, and indicated that we needed to go straight down the highway. She was yelling something, but I couldn't really hear her. I just yelled back, "It's *this* way!"

I was so sure that I *knew* where I was going—but the truth was that I was like a foolish macho man, heading for disaster! We motored on down the freeway a few more miles, got off at the exit I thought was the right one, made a couple of left turns, a right, and all of a sudden it hit me: I had no idea where I was.

I motioned for Diane to follow me into the nearest gas station.

"I'll be right back," I told her, and went into the cashier's office to ask for directions.

The man behind the counter was busily poring over some receipts as I approached.

"Excuse me . . . ."

He looked up.

"Can you tell me how to get to Disneyland?"

"No habla Ingles, senor."

Maybe if I said it slower.

"I said . . . can . . . you . . . tell . . . me . . . ."

He put up his hands to stop me.

"Lo siento. No comprende . . . ."

I turned around and walked outside.

"Well?" Diane asked.

"He doesn't speak English."

"What?" Heavy sigh. "Well, I'm pretty sure it was back . . . ."

"No!" I said, sounding as confident as I possibly could given the circumstances. "It's around here somewhere. I'm sure of it."

"What's around here, Dad?" Jeff wanted to know.

"Oh . . . uh . . . never mind." We still wanted our fun day with Mickey and friends to be a surprise.

I wound up asking for directions at three other businesses in the area, and always with the same result. I didn't know where we were, but *nobody* in this neighborhood spoke English.

Finally, by saying the word, "Dis . . . ney . . . land," as slowly and phonetically as possible, I was able to get the clerk in a convenience store to understand me. The only problem was that I couldn't understand him when he gave me the directions. He tried to do it with hand gestures and so on, but the only thing I could really understand was that we were a long, long way from where we wanted to be.

I was beginning to think that maybe Diane did know something I didn't. Maybe I should swallow my pride and we should head back the way we had come. I managed to find my way back to the freeway, but as we got back on, Diane started making frantic gestures at me. Now what?

She pointed down at her instrument panel and shouted something else. I shook my head because I still couldn't hear her. And then, all of a sudden, there in six lanes of heavy traffic, her bike quit—just like that.

Somehow, we managed to get it pushed over to the right-hand shoulder. I got on and tried to get it re-started. No dice. We tried to get it going by pushing it. That didn't work either.

Finally, I got out an old rope and told Diane that I'd just have to tow her all the way to Hemet. Maybe we could get some help there. So we headed off down the highway, and we made quite a spectacle. Me on my old bike pulling Diane's old bike, both of us with two kids in sidecars, with clothes and camping equipment and so on piled up around us. I'm sure we looked like a biker version of "The Beverly Hillbillies," and I was feeling more and more frustrated and humiliated. People driving by would point at us and laugh. One guy even spent about ten minutes driving alongside of us and taping us with his video camera.

And, to add insult to injury, the rope kept coming untied. That was a terrible, horrible day.

At one point, when the rope came undone for the third time, I threw up my hands and yelled in exasperation, "For crying out loud! All I was trying to do was take my kids to Disneyland!"

"Disneyland? Did you say Disneyland, Dad?"

Now, I'd done it. As if things hadn't already been bad enough, now I'd let the kids know about Disneyland.

"Are we going to Disneyland?"

"Can we go to Disneyland, Dad?"

Even little Misty knew what that meant.

"Mickey Mouse!" she shouted. "Mickey Mouse!"

"No . . . I'm sorry . . . we're not going to Disneyland."

"But why not?"

"Yeah, Dad, why not?"

"Mickey Mouse! Mickey Mouse!"

Let me just say that this was one day I never want to relive. And it wasn't over yet. Somehow, Diane and I managed to get the children to understand that Disneyland was out of the question, at least for now. And we finally got to Hemet.

There, we drove around until I found a motorcycle shop. The mechanic took Diane's bike into the back and, after fifteen minutes or so, came back with the news that it was going to cost $660 to fix. He might as well have been telling me it was going to cost a million dollars. I didn't have anything near $660, and it would take weeks to raise that much money on the road.

"So, you want us to fix it?" he asked.

RIDING THE CROSSROADS

"I . . . Can you let me think about it for awhile?"

"Sure. We'll just keep it here until you make up your mind."

I told Diane that I'd ride on over to the Fitzpatricks and then come back to pick her up. I climbed aboard my motorcycle, pulled on my helmet, turned the ignition and . . . nothing happened. Nothing at all. It was dead. Completely, totally dead.

I just sat there for a moment, feeling shocked. If I was dreaming, this would have been a great time to wake up. But I wasn't. And the mechanic had even worse news for me this time.

"I don't think there's anything I can do for this one," he told me. "It's shot."

He went on to give me a long list of major problems, and considering my motorcycle's age and condition, it wasn't worth it to put that kind of money into it . . . even if I had had money to put into it, which I didn't.

There was nothing to do but call the Fitzpatricks to come pick us up. After that, I had no idea what we were going to do. We were at least 2,000 miles from home. We had maybe one hundred dollars, which wasn't even enough to get us back home on the bus. And, then, too, we had a long series of meetings and other commitments stretched out in front of us. In fact, we were supposed to be in Denver the next week. What did God want us to do? Walk?

While we were waiting for our friends to come pick us up, I wandered around the showroom, looking at all the beautiful new motorcycles. There was one in the show window that particularly caught my eye. It was a beautiful machine. If I could have bought myself whatever I wanted, it would have been perfect—the right color, the right style, everything just right.

Hmmm? Maybe if I called the bank back home and told them about my predicament . . . .

I sought out one of the salesmen.

"I was just wondering, how much would that bike cost me?"

"Which bike is that?"

"That one." I pointed to the beautiful blue machine sitting in the window.

"That one?" He started laughing. "Son . . . you can't afford that bike!"

I could feel my face turning red. I was sure he figured I was just some dumb hick from Arkansas, too stupid to know that a beautiful motorcycle like that was completely out of my reach.

"Besides," he said, "that one's already been sold. In fact, we sold it a couple of weeks ago. The folks who bought it just haven't been in to pick it up yet."

"Herbie?" I looked around to see Dan Fitzpatrick standing in the doorway. "You guys about ready to go?"

We all piled into his car, and all the way to his house I was fuming about the way the salesman had laughed at me.

"I can't believe that guy laughed at me when I asked him about buying that bike."

"What bike was that?" Dan asked.

"Oh, you must have seen it . . . there in the window. Beautiful blue bike. Just beautiful."

Well, the next two days, at the rally there in Hemet, I had to go out and preach about the goodness of God. And that was *not* easy. I was mad at Him . . . and I felt like a hypocrite standing up there and preaching about how good He was. At that particular moment in my life, I was *not* speaking out of personal experience and conviction! Still, responses were good, and several came forward at every service to surrender their hearts to Christ.

RIDING THE CROSSROADS

All the time, I kept wondering what we were going to do about the predicament we were in, and I still didn't have any answers, or any ideas either. That's what I was thinking about as we were all eating lunch at the rally on Saturday—but all I was doing was running the same old non-solutions through my mind, not getting anywhere at all. Suddenly, my thoughts were interrupted by a voice speaking over the loudspeaker. It sounded like Dan Fitzpatrick.

"Will everyone please report to the stage area? And Herbie . . . especially you!"

Diane and I got up, collected the kids, and walked down to the stage area, where a large group of people was already gathered in a big circle. And the first thing I saw was that beautiful blue motorcycle. This *really* took the cake. Whoever had bought that motorcycle had brought it to the rally. What was going on? Wasn't everything that had happened enough, without God rubbing my face in it like this?

Off to the right, Dan Fitzpatrick stood with a microphone in his hand. "Does everybody like this motorcycle?"

Cheers from the crowd.

"How'd you like to own a bike like this?"

More cheers. Louder this time.

"Well, I'm sorry," Dan said, "but you can't have it."

Oohs and ahs and other sounds of disappointment . . . but not *real* disappointment.

And then Dan went on, "And you know why you can't have it? Because it belongs to Herbie!"

What? Had I heard him right.

"Come on over here, Herbie! Take a ride on your new motorcycle!"

A loud, swelling crescendo of cheers went up. And suddenly, all that pent up emotion and frustration just burst inside me. The damn was released, and the tears poured out in a torrent. I think Diane was crying, too, but I'm not sure because I couldn't see through the flood in my own eyes.

Dan put his arm around me. "Herbie," he said, "you remember when I saw you at that rally a couple of months ago?"

I nodded.

"Well, I couldn't believe what you were riding. It wasn't safe. When I came back and told the folks here about it, we just decided we had to get you something better. We love you, brother. And we love you, too, Diane. Now get on your bike and try it out."

The crowd erupted into the longest, loudest cheer of all.

But try as I might, I couldn't ride that bike. Not then. I was too overcome. My knees were so weak I couldn't even hold it up, and I couldn't stop crying. God is so good!

And there was still more to come.

All afternoon, people kept coming up and telling me that they hadn't had an opportunity to give anything toward the purchase of the motorcycle, so they wanted to give something now. Before it was all over, I had been given just over $660. It was enough to get Diane's motorcycle fixed, and we were able to leave for Denver right on schedule!

That was typical of the way God took care of us, although there were times when the miracles had to be forced a little bit.

For example, one time we were in northern Canada, traveling in an area where the towns were very few and far between. It was cold and drizzling, and Diane's bike had run out of gas. That was because her bike wouldn't make it from one town to the next on one tank of gas, pulling both a side car and a trailer.

Now if that wasn't enough of a problem, we were completely out of cash . . . and out of food. I had told the kids when we started out that morning that we'd have honey sandwiches for lunch, and then we'd eat again at the rally that night.

The only thing I knew to do was to ride on to the next town, try to find a way to buy some gas, and then come back and fill Diane's tank. In the meantime, I had no choice but to leave her and the kids bundled up in her sidecar on the side of the road. I figured the nearest town would be perhaps ten miles so I ought to be back well inside of an hour. But it was more like thirty miles. By the time I got there, the drizzle had turned into a steady rain.

Thankfully, there was a bank there, and it was open. But the teller wouldn't cash my check, so I asked to speak to the manager. He was a tall, skinny fellow with close cropped hair, wearing an expensive suit, and thick black-framed glasses that sat far down on his nose. I, on the other hand, was dressed in jeans and leathers, with my long hair hanging down my back. I could tell right away that we were *not* soul brothers.

I told him my predicament and asked if he couldn't please cash a small check for me.

Looking down his nose at me, he said, "I'm sorry, but we cannot cash a check from a bank in the United States."

"But why can't you just call my bank in Arkansas? They'll tell you I have the money in my account."

"Sir," he sniffed, "we will *not* make an international telephone call for you."

"But, but . . . you can just keep the difference. I'll write a check for $50 U.S., and you can give me $50 Canadian."

He just shook his head. "I'm sorry. There's nothing I can do for you."

Meanwhile, back on the side of the road, Diane was beginning to think that maybe I'd just taken off and left her and the kids. I'd been gone over two hours already, and they were freezing. In all the time I'd been gone, they only saw two or three cars go past. At one point, though, a policeman pulled a speeder over to give him a ticket, right across the highway from where Diane was waiting with the kids. She was sure that after he'd taken care of that business, he would at least come over to see if she and the kids were all right. Maybe she could even get him to help out in some way. But he didn't seem interested. Instead, he got back in his car and drove off down the highway, without giving Diane and the kids a second look.

So much, in Diane's mind anyway, for the gallant image of the R.C.M.P.

And back at the bank, I wasn't getting anywhere.

Finally, out of desperation, I played my trump card.

"Look," I told the manger. "If you don't cash my check, I'm just going to stand hear, drip all over your floor, and scare your customers!"

He ignored me for ten or fifteen minutes, hoping that I'd get tired and leave. I half expected the police to come and drag me away. But I was determined that I wasn't going to leave until I got my money . . . and finally, the manager had had enough.

He motioned for me to come up to the counter.

"Okay," he said, "it's worth it to cash your check just to get rid of you! But fifty dollars . . . that's it. Okay?"

"That's great! Thank you!"

"Yeah," he said sarcastically. "You're welcome."

At least three hours had passed by the time I got back to Diane and the kids. But we survived and, as usual, we had a very productive time at the rally.

We had such fun together on the road, growing closer to each other and closer to God through all types of experiences.

One time, we were all involved in the motorcycle games together. I was riding one bike, with Diane as my passenger, and Jeff was piloting another with Randy sitting behind him. In this particular game, the object was for one team to lob a water balloon over a wire that was raised higher and higher with each elimination. The other team's passenger had to catch the balloon without popping it.

As the competition had gone on, Jeff and Randy had become something of a crowd favorite, and now they were going against us in the finals. Diane and I were tough, but the boys were tougher, and they beat us to capture first prize.

After winning, Jeff decided to throw a "victory water balloon" at his mother and me. We saw it coming, and ducked, so that it sailed over our heads. What I didn't know was that a rough and rowdy biker—a guy who had never had any use for me—was standing right behind us. This was a guy who would actually turn away if I tried to talk to him, but he had been standing in the crowd, cheering our boys on to victory.

Well, that balloon hit him head on, drenching him with cold water. He let out a roar that scared birds out of all the surrounding trees. He sounded like a wounded animal, and I figured we were *all* about to feel his wrath. I looked over at Jeff, and he seemed to be rooted to the ground, his face frozen in an expression of shock and horror.

Swallowing the lump that was forming in my throat, I walked over to tell the guy I was sorry, to see if there was anything I could do to make it up to him.

To my amazement, a smile spread across his face and he stuck out his hand.

"Herbie," he said, "I've watched you for years. But today, seeing you out here with your boys . . . well, I just want you to know I think you are 100 per cent. You're all right!"

All of my attempts at talking to this man had failed, but seeing us having fun together as a family had completely changed his mind about me, and that opened the door for the Gospel. I know now that it may have been Jeff who threw that water balloon, but it was God who directed its path.

Within a year, that man and his wife both prayed to ask Jesus into their lives.

At another rally, a woman came to Diane and me in tears, asking if there was anything we could do to help her deal with the grief that was destroying her life. She simply could not come to terms with the death of her son, and she desperately needed God to touch her. While we were praying for her, I opened my eyes and noticed that Randy—who was a very little boy at the time—had has hand on her arm and was praying fervently, as tears of sympathy rolled down his cheeks. His gentle spirit of compassion has touched many hearts over the years.

Often, when the entire family wasn't able to travel together, Randy went with me. Many times he slept sitting upright behind me as we rode together through the night. After we stopped, he would continue to sleep upright until I had put up our tent and could carry him in to the relative comfort of a sleeping bag.

I remember Benji talking to a young man who had come to a secular rally with his grandfather. The boy said he didn't know if he should become a Christian because he didn't know what his grandfather would think about it. "What your grandfather does is up to him," Benji said. "But don't you want to go to heaven? That's where I'm going." Why, yes, as a matter of fact, the boy did want to go to heaven, and Ben led him to saving faith in Jesus on the spot.

A day or two later, Misty led the boy's younger sister to faith in Christ. Misty was still a baby in the early days of our travel together, and she often slept in the nose of the sidecar. She drew many people into conversations with us because they would see her little head—adorned with a tiny motorcycle helmet—pop over the side of the sidecar. They couldn't resist coming over for a closer look, and when they did, it was often easy to talk to them about God.

I remember particularly a rally where two really rough girls had caught Diane's attention and her heart. She tried to talk to them, but they weren't the least bit interested, making their feelings clearly known. But then, when they saw little Misty come along and crawl up into her mom's lap, those two "rough girls" melted. They came over to talk to Misty and her mother, opening the door for Diane to share the Gospel with them. No matter how coarse or crusty someone's exterior may be, little girls always seem to have a way of penetrating through.

Although the kids traveled with us most of the time, we were careful about what we exposed them to, and there were some rallies we would not take them to. One rally in particular stands out in my mind, and it was so wild and wicked, I was sorry almost immediately that I had even brought Diane with me. This was no place for her, and I was worried about her safety.

All around us, people were drunk, some to the point of being sick. Some were dropping acid. Others were smoking dope. And a band was playing the most blasphemous songs I'd ever heard. It was like Sodom and Gommorah come to life, and there was no escaping it. We tried, by going into our tent, unrolling our sleeping bags and attempting to get some sleep. But almost as soon as we were settled, someone fired a shotgun blast right outside. It wasn't a threat—just part of the celebration going on, but it was kind of hard to relax after being jolted by something like that.

What's more, a biker and his old lady started fighting in the tent next to us. They screamed obscenities at each other, threw things, and stomped and smashed around until well after midnight.

And all the time, the band kept playing its blasphemous, nauseating brand of rock'n'roll. Until three in the morning they played, seemingly becoming more outrageous and blasphemous with every new song.

I was lying there listening to all this going on outside and thinking, "I'll never bring Diane to another place like this. I never should have done it in the first place. I won't ever do it again."

Next to me in the darkness, Diane was thinking, "I'll never come to another rally like this. We don't belong here. All we're doing is casting our pearls before swine. What good could we possibly do in a place like this?"

But then, right in the middle of that self-talk, the still, small voice of the Lord spoke to her.

"Now you understand what it was like for me to leave heaven and come to earth," He said.

And there in the darkness, Diane began to cry. I thought she was crying because of the terror outside, but she was crying because God had broken her heart. Because He had filled her with a love for those drunken, hopelessly lost people who were engaged in such evil activities right outside the door of our tent.

I don't know what time we got to sleep, but like I said, it was well after three. And you'd better believe that I got up with an attitude the next morning.

I was surprised when we had a pretty good turnout for our Sunday morning worship service—forty or fifty, I think. But even that wasn't enough to soften my anger.

I figured, "I'll preach my ten-minute sermon, and then we can pack up and get out of here!"

I was preaching from John 3:16, "For God so loved the world," but I sure wasn't feeling a whole lot of love. And then, right in the middle of my sermon, I heard someone start to laugh.

That did it. I didn't care what happened, I wasn't going to put up with this. I turned in the direction of the offender, with every intention of yelling, "Shut up!"

There, sitting on his Harley listening to me, was the biggest, toughest looking biker I had ever seen. If I did tell him to "shut up" he could have broken me like a match stick. But to my surprise, he wasn't laughing. He was crying! Big, wet tears were running down his face, falling into his beard. He was sobbing, loudly and uncontrollably, wiping his eyes with his bandana.

Then I heard someone "over there" begin to laugh. I wheeled in that direction, and the same thing was happening. Another tough biker was so touched by God's love that he, too, had burst into tears. Before I was finished, much of the audience was crying. I knew it wasn't because of my words. It was because the Spirit of God had come into that place. It was an incredible sight. Big, tough, guys fishing around for bandanas or wiping their eyes on their sleeves.

When I gave the invitation at the end of my sermon, at least 10 of these men come forward to say they wanted to surrender to Christ. Many more came and asked for a free copy of the New Testament we were giving out—so many that we didn't have enough Bibles to go around, and that had *never* happened before. One guy kept trying to talk to me, but he couldn't get the words out because he was convulsively crying in sorrow over the sins he had committed.

For me, that was a turning point. A few hours earlier I had been vowing that I would never bring Diane back to another rally like this one. Now, I knew that nothing could keep me away.

I also knew that, even in the midst of the worst sort of

decadence and sin, my family and I were right where God wanted us to be!

Sometimes it seemed that the tougher the time we went through to get to a rally, the more God used us to reach the lost. And sometimes, it wasn't anything we said. There was just something about our presence that seemed to attract people to Him.

That's what happened at a rally in Biloxi, Mississippi. Now, this rally is so wild that there are official signs posted at the entrances, reminding those who are leaving the grounds to put their clothes on before they venture into town. It is one of the wildest environments I've ever visited, and it would be hard to describe how it can wear you out spending four days trying to witness for Christ in a place like that. Almost every year, I vow that I will never return, and every year, the Spirit of Christ reminds me that yes, I will return, because there will be people here next year, just as there were this year, who need Him.

One year, one of the ones who needed Him was a young guy who was prospecting with one of the outlaw groups. In fact, he had just received his patch, which he was wearing proudly—and he didn't want to have anything at all to do with CMA. At one point, some of our men tried to talk to him, and he stumbled all over himself trying to get away from them. He didn't want his brothers to see him even *talking* to us.

Even so, all during the rally, he kept watching us. And then on Saturday afternoon, he left the rally early. Somewhere between Biloxi and Jackson, he pulled over to the side of the road and ripped the outlaw patch from his jacket.

Then he went to the nearest Harley shop and asked if anyone there knew anything about the Christian Motorcyclists Association.

"As a matter of fact, yes, I do," the owner said. "I've got some customers who belong to CMA, and I can give you their phone number if you'd like."

"I'd appreciate that."

It turned out that the CMAers he knew were an older "aunt and uncle" type who were just sitting down to dinner when the young man called.

After he explained why he was calling, the woman said, "You're not far from us. Why don't you come over and have a bite with us?"

"You sure?"

"Oh, yes. Come on over. We'd love to have you."

He took them up on the offer—he was delighted to have a home-cooked meal—and in the course of dinner he said, "You know, I've just gone through all of these things to become an outlaw. And then I was so excited about going to my first event as a member of the group. But when I was there, all I could think about was how much more fun the Christians were having than we were."

He said, "We were all sitting around *trying* to have fun. But we weren't, really. But the Christians . . . man . . . I wish I could enjoy life like that."

That evening meal was the beginning of a long relationship with that young man, who eventually became a Christian, and is now an active member of CMA!

At another rally, we donated some Christian music tapes to be given as a door prize, and everyone who won one eventually established a relationship with CMA.

I remember one woman in particular. Even though I'm ashamed to admit it, I found myself cringing inside when she won the tape. For one thing, she couldn't seem to open her mouth without letting some sort of obscenity slip out. And for another, she was wearing one of the skimpiest outfits I have ever seen.

Naturally, she thought it was really funny when she won one of our prizes. She sashayed up on stage to get it, and then made a big joke out of it, "Ooooh! God music! How *wonderful!* "

Then, she threw the tape into the cab of her husband's truck and forgot all about it. A few days later, when he was on his way to work, her husband happened to see it lying there. He thought he'd pop it into the tape player, just to see what it was like. He figured that maybe it would be good for a laugh or something. But instead, the tape started off with a really kicking version of *God's Not Dead*, and he found that the music and the lyrics kept replaying through his head all day long. On the way home that night, he decided to listen to the rest of the tape. In fact, he listened to it for several days as he drove back and forth to work.

As he was on his way home one Wednesday night, he passed a little white church building. And as he did, he knew that he wanted to understand the reality of the music he had been listening to. The way this guy looked at the time would have been a scary sight to see him walking toward you. And I imagine the preacher in that little church had quite a shock when someone knocked on the door of his office, and he opened it to find that big, burly biker dude standing there.

"Ye . . . .yes?"

"Preacher . . . I've been listening to this tape that says He paid a debt He didn't owe because I owned a debt I couldn't pay. Can you help me understand what that means?"

"I certainly can."

Later that evening, when he arrived home, that biker had a surprise for his wife. He walked into the house with tears running down his cheeks and said, "I want you to know that I've just committed my life to the Lord. And that's not all. There are some things I have to tell you?"

"What things?"

He took her hands in his. "It hurts me to tell you this, but I have to." Then he went on to tell her of numerous times during their marriage when he had failed her and let her down as a husband. He concluded by saying, "If you want to leave me now, I'll understand, and you're free to go. But I'll always take care of you. And if you'll forgive me, I know I can love you now like I've never loved you before."

Of course it hurt her to hear his confession, but instead of walking away, she pulled him close and cried, "I forgive you. And I want what you've got."

That night, he took her back to that little church and the preacher led her to the Lord. They were both baptized, and the last time I saw them, they were both very actively involved in the ministry of that congregation.

And then, there was the miracle named Jack.

I was in a motorcycle shop having some work done on my bike, and one of the guys told me he had something he wanted to show me. He pulled his wallet out of the back pocket, drew out a piece of paper, unfolding it carefully, as if it were something precious, and handed it to me, saying, "Have you ever seen anything like this?"

I nodded, "Yes . . . I have." It was one of CMA's tracts, "Jesus Would Have Ridden a Harley."

"Well, I've carried this one around for a couple of months. Sure wish I knew where I could get some more."

"I think I can get you some."

"Could you? That would be great?"

During the course of our conversation, I found out the guy's name was Jack. He was a long-time member of one of the largest and best known rowdy-type groups in the area. He wasn't a Christian, but the tract had at least led him to think about spiritual realities, and as soon as I got back home, I sent several copies to him.

Over the next few months, I made several trips back to that shop and always made a point to stop and talk with Jack. He seemed happy to see me, and was as polite as could be. But he refused to get serious about his relationship with God. I also talked to Charles Hale, one of our directors, and asked him to go by and talk to Jack. I knew that with persistence we could get him into the kingdom.

Then one day, Charles called to say that Jack was facing very serious open heart surgery. Doctors had told him there was about a 50-50 chance that he'd make it through the operation—and he was scared. He had asked Charles to pray with him, and he had done so, asking specifically for healing.

A few days after getting the phone call from Charles, I got another one from Jack's wife, "I'm calling to tell you that God is alive and well!"

"What?"

"Jack doesn't need surgery!"

"He doesn't? Praise God!"

"You said it! Praise God!"

It seems that Jack had gone back into the hospital for some tests, and his doctor found that the life-threatening heart problem had apparently "healed itself." He was so astounded by this that he called in several other doctors to confirm his findings, and they all agreed. Jack did not need the surgery that, just a few weeks before, had been considered absolutely essential.

Well, you'd better believe that Jack surrendered his life to Christ—and for the next several months, he witnessed to everyone who came into that motorcycle shop where he worked. He'd corner one of the customers and say, "Sit down. I want to tell you a story." The story itself would start with the tract and wind up with Jack's healing, and a glowing description of how happy he was now that Christ had come into his life."

On one of my visits to that shop, I heard Jack start in with somebody, "Sit down. I want to tell you a story." And the mechanic who was working on my bike smiled and said, "I've heard that story so many times."

I smiled, too. I was glad Jack was so excited about his new-found faith.

About six months later, Jack went to a gun show—guns being something he had always loved *almost* as much as motorcycles. He was sitting in a hot tub with a buddy, just having a great time, when he leaned back with a big smile on his face—and died. There was no struggle. Apparently no pain. He was in this world one moment, and then he had gone on to the next.

When I got the news, I was afraid his wife would feel that God had let her down and that she would be tempted to walk away from Him. I shouldn't have worried.

She said, "Herbie, Jack had six months he never would have had . . . and they were a wonderful six months. For the first time in his life, he knew what life was all about. We both did. And you know what? It means so much to me to know that he died with a smile on his face."

Then she told me that she wanted me to conduct his funeral.

Of course, I told her I would be honored. I took a bunch of those "Jesus Would Have Ridden a Harley" tracts with me, hoping that I'd find a way to pass them out.

The funeral itself was a most interesting experience. There were at least 150 Harleys parked in front of the funeral home that day, and the whole hierarchy of his club sat right up front. I wanted to get through to these rough, tough, guys, but I knew I needed to be cautious. If you try to hit guys like that over the head with the Gospel, they tend to hit back.

So, looking out over that gathering of weather-beaten faces of beards and hair, of tattooed arms and chests, I started off by talking about some of the things that Jack loved.

"You know," I said, "Jack just *loved* Harleys."

"Yeah, yeah!"

"And Jack loved guns."

"Damn straight!"

"And Jack loved to tell stories."

By that time, they all knew that I really knew Jack, and that gave me some credibility.

"And in the last months of his life, Jack came to love Jesus. He loved Jesus because he knew that Jesus loved him."

I pulled the tract out of my pocket. "Let me read you something that meant a lot to Jack."

As I read that tract, putting as much feeling into it as I possibly could, I began to see a few tears here and there falling down the cheeks of some of those tough-looking faces.

When I finished, I said, "Some of you are going to leave here today and you'll never see Jack again. You're going to put him in the ground, and that will be it. But as for me, well, *I* know I'm going to see him again . . . because I know I'll see him in heaven."

At that, I invited the mourners to file by the casket and pay their respects to their friend. I wanted to hand out the tracts then, but something held me back. It just didn't seem that the time was right.

After that, we all went out to the cemetery, which is where the club took over. They have a rule that "no man can ever throw dirt in a brother's face." So what they did was give a shovel to Jack's son—who was also a member of the group—and allowed him to put the first shovelful of dirt on the casket. After this, they passed around a bottle of whiskey, allowed me to say another few words, and then it was time to leave.

I still had all those tracts with me, but I'd never had a chance to pass them out. Then, just as I was ready to leave, someone tapped me on the shoulder. I turned around to see a biker girl . . . someone's "old lady," barely out of her teens, if that old. She was wearing a back patch that marked her as "property of" someone.

"Hey, Preacher," she said, "you got any more of those stories that Jack liked?"

"Oh, sure," I said. I've got a lot of them."

"Well," she looked almost shy. "Do you think you could let me have some. I know some people here'd like to have one."

Of course, I gave her all I had . . . and the last thing I saw, as I drove away from the cemetery, was that little "biker chick" surrounded by bikers, all of whom were clamoring for a copy of our tract.

"Jack," I whispered as I drove away, "I have a very good feeling that a whole lot of your brothers are going to be seeing you again!"

CHAPTER 15

Weekend Warriors

Diane and the kids were on the road with me for most of three years . . . three terrific years I wouldn't change for the world. They were years of tremendous spiritual growth for all of us.

I will never know how Diane managed to keep the kids current on their math, English and other schoolwork and still spend 35,000-plus miles a year on the road—but she did.

Some well-meaning friends told us we were wrong for doing what we were doing, not only because it was depriving the kids of developing normal relationships with other children their ages, but because it was exposing them to the seamier side of life. Weren't we worried, they wanted to know, about the kids being attracted to the biker lifestyle? And what about their personal safety?

We understood those concerns. And, of course, when we went to some of the roughest secular rallies, we worried a bit about what might happen to the kids since we couldn't be there to watch them every minute. Basically, the advice we gave them was to trust their hearts and their consciences as they attempted to be sensitive to the leading of the Holy Spirit. That advice never failed them.

Certainly, they saw the seamier side of the biker life, but hardly in a way that seemed attractive. They saw their share of people who were drunk or stoned or beaten down by life. But seeing some drunk guy throwing up on his boots is hardly appealing.

I remember how, at one rally, my kids were very amused at first when a bunch of drunk men crowded into a small plastic wading pool and began singing, *Rubber Duckie.* But then, after awhile, their amusement began to turn to embarrassment. And when I talked to them about it later, they all told me how happy they were that that wasn't their Dad out there.

None of the kids had ever seemed to have any difficulty making friends, and it was thrilling for Diane and me to see them lead some of those friends to the Lord.

One time, the kids made friends with a youngster from Bangkok, telling him all about Jesus and how much He meant to them. At the end of their time together, the young man was sad that he had to return home and leave his newfound friends. "And besides," he told them, "Jesus isn't in Thailand."

"Well, why not take Him with you?" my kids asked. And that's exactly what he did!

As I said, these were times of tremendous growth and excitement for my family, and they were also times of growth and excitement for CMA as a whole.

When I came on board there were about 20,000 members involved in 200 CMA chapters all over the country, and more people were coming into the organization all the time. For administrative purposes, the country had been divided into five regions, every region with its own evangelist, but for the most part, the organization was fairly loose and disorganized. Dad's calling had always been that of an evangelist, and it was not his place nor his forte to worry overly much about things like organization and structure. In that respect, he was very much like the Apostles, who appointed deacons to be in charge of administrative duties so that they themselves could devote themselves fully to the preaching of the Word.

Anyway, the evangelists were pretty much on their own. They just went out and preached the Gospel. There was no coordination of effort, no working with other groups. There had always been a newsletter, beginning way back. It started out as a mimeographed effort which my mother wrote, printed, addressed and mailed out to the membership. (Today, that newsletter, "The Heartbeat" continues, going out monthly to our active membership.) But other than that, there was no concerted effort to work with the members at large, and, as I traveled across the country, I began to see how important that was. Unless we had more structure, things were going to unravel.

My father and CMA's board of directors agreed with me, and they asked me to assume the job of administrator. As administrator, I still did quite a bit of teaching and training, but I also began the task of giving the Christian Motorcyclists Association a cohesive national policy and structure.

For example, we had never really defined what a CMA chapter was, and as I rode around the country I could sense that a lot of our chapters were becoming nothing more than Christian ride groups. To remedy this situation, we put together our first guideline books explaining what a chapter is and does. We didn't ask anything unreasonable, just that chapters have a function and a purpose—that they have the same heartbeat that brought CMA into existence. Evangelism. Sharing the love of Jesus.

Our definition of a CMA chapter is that it is a group of people who are the hands of CMA, expressing the heart of CMA to the local community.

It was at this time that we also started having "Seasons of Refreshing" conferences every winter. First, one in a region, and then two, and now one in each state. We use these conferences to restate our purpose, to renew the minds of the old members, and to explain to the new members what CMA is all about. We train people in what we call "hands-on evangelism," and we seek to build enthusiasm for the programs and purposes of the Christian Motorcyclists Association. This has unified us as we have grown and kept evangelism in the forefront of what we do.

I'm often asked what a person would have to do to start a CMA chapter in his or her community. The answer is that if you call our national office, we'll send a state coordinator to come and meet with you. He will tell you in detail what CMA is all about. He will explain the responsibilities of CMA chapters. And, he will help you decide if you and your group have the same heart for evangelism that guides CMA.

If a mutual decision is made that your group should become a part of CMA, he will provide posters and classified ads that can be used to invite people to an organizational meeting. He will also give some information that can be put into church bulletins in your area. Then, before you can be officially designated as a CMA chapter, you must have at least 10 people who meet together for six months. After that time, if the coordinator and the regional evangelist agree, you will receive your charter as a CMA chapter. There are no dues or membership fees.

We also sought to put a more structured "chain of command" into place, not to build a hierarchy, but so the organization can move forward in a greater degree of unity in our efforts to bring others into God's kingdom.

On the national level, there is the president and the board of directors. After that, there are the on-staff regional evangelists who oversee the different regions of the United States and the state coordinators. From there, depending upon the geography and the population of the state involved, we have field reps and lay evangelists. These men and women are volunteers who are trained to go and represent CMA at secular events. Many of them work full-time at other jobs, but they may also spend 16 to 25 weekends a year at various motorcycle rallies. These are "weekend warriors" who love the Lord and will do whatever they can to serve Him.

And then there is the part of our ministry that was developed by one of our lay evangelists and his wife—one of my very favorite parts of CMA, the ministry teams. We have nine ministry teams—hospitality, mechanical, servant's, first-aid, children's, women's, prayer, prison, and music. The people who are involved in these teams go through an annual training where they learn how to witness through the platform of whatever skills, talents and gifts they may have.

There may be a guy who, if asked to get up at a rally and give his testimony, would stammer and stumble and maybe even end up running for cover. He just couldn't do it. But maybe he's a mechanic, and he can learn to feel comfortable talking to people about the Lord while he's working on their bikes. We have a lot of people like this on our various ministry teams. They never thought they were capable of one-to-one evangelism, but they're finding out that's not so, and you should see how excited they are when they lead someone into God's kingdom!

When a person joins one of these ministry teams, he's making a one-year commitment. He goes through a series of tapes where he learns what to do at a rally, what not to do, how to start up a conversation with someone, etc. You see, we do not believe in going into a rally and preaching to strangers, or just randomly handing out tracts. That won't work. We believe in building relationships.

We believe in showing the love of Christ by serving others. That's why we provide emergency services to those who are experiencing mechanical trouble. That's why we come to the aid of those who need minor emergency medical help. In this way, we win people's respect and trust, and then they are more likely to listen when we try to tell them about the salvation that can be obtained through faith in Christ.

Even the simple matter of giving a cup of cold water to someone who is thirsty can help to build a relationship. And that's why, over the last few years we have given away 15 to 20,000 gallons of water, every drop of it in eight-ounce cups. We call them Gospel cups because they have the plan of salvation printed on them.

If you've ever been to a rally like Sturgis, you know what it means to be hot, tired and thirsty. It gets so hot out there that you can find some people selling small cups of water for $1.50 a piece and finding hundreds of customers willing to pay that price.

Naturally, when people find out they can get water free from CMA, they like us a lot. We sometimes have literally hundreds of people waiting in line for water—and they *do* read the message printed on those cups.

For example, one of our couples was riding through Tennessee when they saw another motorcyclist broken down by the side of the road. They stopped to see if they could be of assistance, and, at one point, the woman said, "Let me tell you what we're all about."

"Lady," the guy said, "you don't have to tell me what you're all about."

And then, reaching down into his saddlebag, he fished out one of our cups.

He went on to tell her that he was on his way home to face charges of some kind and was carrying one of our cups for good luck. That was his concept of Christianity—that it consisted of artifacts that might possibly bring you good fortune. But right there on the side of the road, our couple led that young man to Christ, and then they referred him to CMA members in California, who were able to minister to him and stand with him as he faced his day in court. That young man's life has been changed—and it all started with a cup of cold water.

Our people also build relationships at rallies by helping to run races, working gates, controlling the parking, working their tails off. They work long hours in scorching summer heat. They go home exhausted, splattered with mud, covered with dust. But all of that hard work lets people know that we are serious about showing the love of Jesus, and they respond.

At Sturgis, we also bought benches, on which the CMA logo was clearly painted, and set them up all along the main street there. I've spent quite a bit of time just sitting on one of those benches and witnessing to people who happened to come along—and let me tell you, people are *grateful* for those benches. Right away, they like us because of what we've done, and then they're ready and willing to talk . . . and listen.

In one two-hour period on one occasion, I witnessed to people from three countries in Europe as well as from all over the United States. That happened just because there was a place for people to "sit down and take a load off."

Along with the gospel cups, the benches, and our other "service-oriented" ways of preaching the Gospel, we have also produced a number of very successful tracts.

One is called, "Let Those Who Ride Decide." The title refers to the widely debated issue of choice with regard to the wearing of safety helmets. But our tract points out that there is another, even more important choice for bikers to make—and that is whether or not to accept Christ's offer of salvation.

We also have a tract that talks about the fact that you don't throw away a bike just because something goes wrong, and neither should you trash Christianity just because someone has let you down.

Our number one tract, though, is still, "Jesus Would Have Ridden a Harley." This tract helps bikers who have felt rejected begin to identify with the love of Christ.

Our art director, Jimmy Pineda, has done a marvelous job on these tracts, giving them a modern, fresh look that appeals to today's generation.

Jimmy has also put together a number of terrific ads which have been placed in national motorcycle magazines.

The first ad was called "Still Time to Change the Road You're On," and the response was overwhelming. When Desert Storm occurred, we hurriedly got an ad ready that spoke to that situation. What we didn't know, though, was that God was going to use one of our old advertisements with tremendous effect among our soldiers in Saudi Arabia. What happened was that hundreds of old magazines were shipped to our soldiers there, including many motorcycle magazines containing our, "Still Time to Change the Road You're On" ad. As a result, we received more than 500 responses to that ad alone from our soldiers who were fighting in Desert Storm.

To all who responded, we sent an audio tape featuring a verbal presentation of the Gospel and how to grow with the Lord, along with a copy of our modern-language New Testament which we call a "Life's Manual." So we wound up sending more than 500 Bibles into Saudi Arabia, and many of the people who accepted the Lord over there are now leaders in CMA here at home.

I think the best ad we've ever done was called "Second Look." This ad features a closeup of the handlebars of a motorcycle, including the rear-view mirror, and in that mirror is the reflection of Jesus on the cross. Also on the mirror are printed the words, "Objects in mirror may be closer than they appear." That ad has generated a huge response, and the owners of one of the best-known motorcycle magazines asked us if they could "please" have the original artwork. We found out later that they had a huge plaque made of that ad, and they have it hanging in a prominent position in their offices. And the owners of that magazine are *not* Christians.

These are just some of the various means we use to spread the Gospel. But the effectiveness of all of these things depends upon the personal relationships we build with others. None of these things would work if the people "out there" didn't know that we were always willing to serve and help. We train our people not to make "projects" out of "lost souls," but to build loving relationships—to go to motorcycle events as motorcyclists who love motorcycling. Through letting their Christian light shine in their actions and relationships, they earn the right to speak for Him and be heard.

A few years ago in Daytona Beach, just before "Bike Week," a biker—a member of an outlaw group—was shot and killed, and some of our people went to his funeral. Outside, as the mourners were leaving, the police swept in, ordered everybody onto the ground and started checking for weapons. Some of the outlaw guys were indignant that the CMAers were also being treated this way.

"Hey! Those guys are Christians. They're not with us. Let 'em go."

"Shut up and stay down!" came the response.

And so, the Christian bikers spent 45 minutes with their faces in the dirt, after which they were taken downtown and booked into jail. It was several hours before they were finally cleared and released.

A few days later, we received official notice from the leaders of the outlaw group involved. It said, "Your guys have been down in the dirt with us. You're welcome in our gatherings *any* time."

Once again, some gospel seeds had been planted.

We have faith, strengthened by past experience, that those seeds will produce a bountiful harvest.

CHAPTER 16

Run for the Son

It was sometime in early 1987. I was riding alone through West Texas in a terrible rain storm. I was miserable in just about every way it's possible for a person to be miserable. I was wet. I was cold. I was tired. And I wanted to be home.

My mind was really focused on my own misery. I certainly wasn't thinking too much about God at the time, even though He was the reason I was out there on that motorcycle in such a terrible rainstorm in the first place. But suddenly, a vision straight from heaven burned into my brain. I saw the entire world, as if I was looking at it from outer space, and a circle made of motorcycles stretched all the way around it.

It seemed clear that God was telling me that he wanted CMA to have an annual event that would raise money for missions work around the world. The gloomy, miserable state of mind was gone, and I was elated with the joy of the Lord. And so that night, instead of sleeping like anyone would normally do after a hard, rainy day like that, I stayed up making notes on a napkin, figuring out how the whole thing would be put together.

When I got home a few days later, my dad had just arrived from a trip to Canada. It was rare that we were both in town at the same time, so I called and asked him to meet me at a restaurant for breakfast. Over our pancakes and bacon I told him about the vision I'd seen, and when I did, he smiled and said, "You know . . . I had a dream about the very same thing." Well, that was all the confirmation I needed to know this was something from the Lord.

So when we were done with our breakfast, I went to my office, got a blank piece of paper and started writing out more specific details for an event that was to become known as the "Run for the Son," an event that has aided missions efforts all around the world.

The idea is to have motorcyclists find people who will sponsor them—pay a certain amount of money for every mile they ride. There is nothing really unique about the idea. This is something motorcyclists do all the time to raise money for various charitable organizations. The difference was that instead of raising funds to support an organization that was looking for answers, we would invest in the answer we had already found—Jesus Christ.

CMA has always been very missions-oriented. Every quarter we take ten per cent of our undesignated funds and send them to various mission outreaches. So in a way, the Run for the Son was just an extension of that.

But when I first brought up the idea, some of the board members thought that maybe I had been out riding in the sun too long. And, to be honest, I really hadn't given a lot of thought to the coordination efforts or the logistics that would be required to turn a dream of this magnitude into a reality.

Basically, the board told me to get my plans in better shape and come back later.

Naturally, I was terribly disappointed. But I wasn't about to give up on the idea. Instead, I spent a lot of time over the next six months fleshing out my plans, and then I went back to the board. This time they bought the idea, although I have to say that the approval wasn't entirely enthusiastic.

There was some nervousness, and I couldn't blame anyone for that.

The first order of business was to print up flyers and brochures explaining the event, as well as registration and sponsorship forms. When the printing bill for all of these materials came in it was nearly $10,000, and I almost had a heart attack. I think Roy Johnson's heart really did skip a few beats when he saw that bill.

He called me immediately, and it seemed to me that his voice had risen an octave or two.

"Herbie . . . have you seen this bill?"

"Uh . . . yeah . . . Roy. I'm the one who passed it on to you."

"But . . . I've . . . we've never had a bill this big."

"Yeah, it's a whopper, isn't it?" I tried to smile.

"Well . . . what am I supposed to do with it?"

"Pay it?" I asked.

"How?"

"I don't know. We'll just have to look for a way."

It wasn't easy but we did manage to find enough money to pay the bill . . . but by this time I was beginning to doubt, at least a little bit, the vision that had started this whole business. I sure hoped I had been hearing from God. If this Run for the Son thing didn't take off, we were out a whole lot of money.

Over the next few weeks I began to doubt myself even more, because the over-all response from the CMA chapters was not a very good one. At least, the responses I heard were not very good. People were wondering what was going on. They weren't sure they wanted to be involved. It got so bad that I started refusing to answer the phone because I didn't want to hear any more complaints.

There seemed to be three main reasons why people were skeptical regarding The Run for the Son. First, because it was so different from anything we had done before. Second, some people were having trouble with the idea of trying to raise money for foreign missions because we had always focused our attention on evangelism here at home. Third, some were worried about giving so much money away when our own budget was so tight—so tight, in fact, that the organization's very survival was in question.

More than one of our field reps had serious doubts about the logic behind the event, one even telling me that he didn't think he could support it for spiritual reasons. He just didn't think it was a proper way to raise money. I told him that if that was the way he felt, then I didn't want him to do anything to support the event. I was not about to ask him to do something that would hurt his conscience toward God. A few days after I spoke to him, he called and told me that after a lot of serious praying, he had come to the conclusion that the Lord was indeed behind it. As it turned out, he became one of the event's biggest supporters.

When the printing was finally ready, I went over to pick it up, and that gave me a better idea of the magnitude of what we were trying to do. I couldn't begin to fit it all in the trunk of my car. There was so much paper that it completely filled our garage and kitchen. For three months we did not eat at our kitchen table because it was piled high with all those printed materials.

Among that huge stack of paper were 75,000 receipts that had to be counted out one-by-one in stacks of fifteen and sent them out. Diane, the kids, and I spent countless hours collating, folding, licking and addressing envelopes. To this day, Jeff will joke that, "When I was born, you took me home and said, 'Son, here . . . put this letter in this envelope.'" That's not quite true. Almost. But not quite.

Misty was a little too young to be of much help, since she was still in preschool, but she did what she could. We got one letter back from a man who said, "Now I see just what a grassroots organization this is. My letter had Legos in it." Courtesy of Misty, no doubt.

As the day of the first run approached, May 7, 1988, I would have stopped it if I could have. The day of the run I got up sick to my stomach from the stress I was feeling. I was afraid it was going to fail, and that meant that I was going to fail because I had pushed so hard for it.

The Arkansas group was going to meet at Mount Magazine, which is the highest point in the state. We had a call-in station set up where people from throughout the country could call, give their chapter name, and tell us how much they had raised. Our goal was to have each chapter raise $1,000, which would have been a nationwide total of $250,000. We had decided that we were going to use 20 per cent of that money to buy motorcycles for native pastors in Third World countries, 40 per cent to buy Bibles for closed countries, which would be distributed through Brother Andrew's organization, Open Doors, and the final 40 per cent for home missions. None of the money was to go into the day-to-day administration of CMA.

Before I left home that morning I called in to see what was being reported from our East Coast chapters. The news I got didn't help my nervousness because it was nothing to jump up and down about. A few hundred dollars had come in, but that wasn't much from an entire region of the country.

On my way up the mountain, I even stopped at a pay phone to make another call to check on the total. By this time, it was up to a few thousand dollars. That made me feel better. We might not make enough money to buy a whole lot of motorcycles or Bibles, but if this held up, we would at least make enough to pay off our printing bill.

By the time I got to our call-in area, almost exactly enough money had come in to pay that bill, and additional calls were arriving at a steady pace. They came from New York, Florida, Colorado, New Mexico and California. Motorcyclists all over the country were getting into it. I began to feel ashamed of myself for worrying so much about it. This had always been God's idea . . . not mine . . . and God is always faithful.

By the time we heard from the last West Coast participants, around 10:00 that night, we had raised just under $200,000! That was short of our goal, but it was a great start —much more than most had anticipated raising!

Every year since then the Run for the Son has been held on the first Saturday in May, and over the years we have raised millions of dollars and given away every penny of it to spread the Gospel. We have given away hundreds of motorcycles and bicycles and we have provided thousands of Bibles to Christians in places like China and the former Soviet Union.

We've even bought motorcycles out from under Fidel Castro that he couldn't afford to keep and gave them to Cuban pastors.

I had the personal privilege of going to Cuba to present bikes and motorcycles to several pastors there. Bob Hawley, who came from Open Doors to take over as administrator of CMA after I assumed the post of president, went with me.

On the evening of the big occasion, I was sitting in the back of a car with Bob as we motored our way into the grounds of the seminary where the presentations were to take place. I noticed, when we drove past some of the pastors who were standing in the parking lot, that one of them suddenly covered his mouth and pointed in my direction.

"Did you see that?" Bob asked. "That guy looks like he just saw a ghost."

"Yeah, I wonder what's going on."

As I got out of the car, I could feel him staring at me—a middle-aged Cuban gentleman with a small mustache, a weather-beaten face, and clutching a very well-worn Bible. A woman wearing a neat but ragged house dress was standing next to him—his wife, I guessed—and he put his arm around her, pulling her close to him as he pointed at me and talked excitedly to her in Spanish. I didn't know what was going on, but there was something about me that he found startling, surprising. He almost looked frightened.

Later, after all of the presentations had been made, he worked his way to the front and began talking excitedly in Spanish, pointing at my hair, which seemed to have some special significance. Our translator was working as hard as he could, because the fellow was talking at about the same speed that Nolan Ryan can throw a fastball. At one point, he started crying, and we had to wait several minutes for him to regain his composure so he could continue.

Finally, we managed to get him calmed down enough to where the translator could understand what he was trying to say. He told us that just a few weeks earlier he had become so discouraged that he had angrily told the Lord he was on the verge of walking away from the ministry.

"God, I committed my life to You! My wife and my children have committed their lives to You. But it seems to me that You're not doing your part.

"We don't have food to eat. We can't get food coupons like others do because I'm a pastor. My children can't play on the playground because I'm a pastor. If I was doing another job, we'd be much better off. I could be giving my family a better life."

And then he said, "If You don't show me that You're with

me—that I'm doing what You want me to do, I'm just going to quit!"

He thought about what he had said for a few minutes and then said, "God, if You're who You say You are, then I want You to give me a bicycle! No, wait a minute . . . if You're God, give me a motorcycle."

Up until that time, the man had been borrowing a bicycle from a man in his church to take care of his duties as a pastor. The bicycle was old and rickety but, when it was available, it was the only means of transportation he had.

That night, when the pastor told his wife that he had asked the Lord to give him a motorcycle, she shook her head and laughed at him.

"What would you do with a motorcycle? You've never even been on a motorcycle! You don't know how to ride one! Besides . . . you're afraid of them!"

"That's all right. I'll learn. Just think of what I could do If I had a motorcycle."

At his next Sunday morning worship service, he asked everyone to be praying with him that God would give him a motorcycle. That was really asking for a miracle, especially in his little village in one of the poorest parts of Cuba. But He figured that if God owned the cattle on a thousand hills, He also owned the motorcycles in a thousand salesrooms.

A few days later, he received a telegram from one of our people in Havana, asking him to come to the city for a meeting on a certain date. The telegram didn't say why he was supposed to come to Havana. It didn't even hint at a reason. But because it was signed by someone he knew to be a Christian, he decided right away that he and his wife would do whatever they could to make the trip. They had to travel for several days—on bus and on foot—to get to Cuba's capital city. And still, they had no idea what to expect once they got there.

One night as he and his wife were walking along the highway, he had a vision in which he saw a man with long, gray hair and heard the Lord say, "This is a Christian. He's my son. I love him, and he's going to come and meet your need."

The pastor shook his head. "No, Lord. He can't be a Christian. He has long hair, and a Christian can't have long hair."

But he felt God's voice saying again, more emphatically this time, "This is my son . . . my servant. I am well pleased with him. And he is coming to help you."

He still wasn't convinced that anyone who had long hair could be a Christian. Had he really heard from God, or had he started seeing and hearing things because he was so exhausted from his long trip?

He didn't know what to think.

And then, as he and his wife had stood in the seminary parking lot on that early fall morning, still not really knowing why they had been asked to come to Havana, our car had driven by, and he had seen my "long, gray hair" through the rear window.

Through the interpreter, and through his tears, he said, "You were the one in that vision. It was your long hair I saw! It was your face I saw! It was you God sent to help me! And now I have my motorcycle! Praise God, I have my motorcycle!"

His wife stood off in the distance, seemingly too shy to get any closer, but I could see that she, too, was crying. And, after hearing the story her husband had to tell, my eyes, too, were filled with tears.

That night in my hotel room I got down on my knees and said, "Lord, thank you for allowing me to be a part of this. Forgive me if we've ever been tempted to think that the Run for the Son was *my* idea. This has been your idea all the way, Lord. I see that so clearly now."

With God's continued blessing, the Run for the Son will be an important part of CMA for many years to come.

CHAPTER 17

Home at Last

Mom was never the same after her accident in 1982.

There were little things that just weren't right. Her coordination and depth perception seemed to be off. She'd stumble sometimes.

She always tried to laugh it off. "I don't know what's wrong with me. I'm getting so clumsy!"

We chalked it all up to her accident and hoped that it would get better with time.

But it didn't. Instead, as time went by, Kelly, my Dad and I all had to admit that it was getting worse, not better.

We urged her to see a doctor, but she balked at the idea. "It's no big deal," she'd say. "I'm just getting old."

"Mom," I argued. "You're 53 years old. That's *not* old."

Finally, because the rest of us wouldn't leave her alone, she agreed to go in and have some tests done. What she hadn't told us was that things were really worse than we knew. And even though she didn't let on, she was scared and with good reason.

I don't remember where I was, somewhere on the road as usual, when Dad called with the news. Mom had been diagnosed with multiple sclerosis. I wasn't sure, at the time, what that meant, but I knew it wasn't good. Of course, I had heard of multiple sclerosis, but I didn't really know anything about it.

Dad went on to explain that the doctor said there was no

treatment, nor any hope that things would get better. Some time within the next year or two, Mom would probably start needing a walker to get around. After that, she would be confined to a wheelchair, and then to complete bed-rest as the disease progressed. Doctors told him that, based on their tests, my mother had a particularly fast-moving form of MS. Although the disease is always progressive and irreversible, in some cases there can be years of relatively good health. Mom's doctors did not expect this to be the case with her.

She took the bad news the way she always handled any type of adversity—with calm good humor. As for Dad, he planned to stay on the road, "until the time comes when she needs me to be here with her. You know," he said, "she wouldn't have it any other way."

I knew he was right. CMA was every bit as important to her as it was to my father. She loved everything about the organization, and she was not about to give it up until she absolutely had to.

Not too long after I got the news about Mom, I was preaching at a rally in Canada. It was one of those times when I couldn't wait for the rally to be over so I could get home. I was terribly homesick. I missed Diane and the kids, and, then, too, the news about Mom only added to the feeling that I was indeed a long, long way from home.

I knew that if I rode as long and hard as I could, I'd be home inside of two days, and that's what I decided to do. I hadn't counted on the fact that God had other plans.

Somewhere in the southern part of North Dakota, my bike started skipping—and that's really too mild of a description. One moment it was running fine, and the next it was burping and bucking and acting quite a bit like a particularly cranky horse I had known in my younger days.

I had no idea what could cause that sort of behavior to

come on all of a sudden. If I had been anywhere else, I might have tried to go on anyway, that's how badly I wanted to get home. But there wasn't another town for at least 100 miles—nothing but Indian Reservation stretched out in front of me—and if I got stranded out there, who knew when I'd get home? I was tempted, but I knew I really couldn't take the risk.

I took the next exit, hiccupped my way to the nearest motel, got a room for the night, and asked the clerk if there was a motorcycle shop in town.

He scratched his head for a moment. "No . . . sorry . . . but the nearest one I can think of is . . . ." and he named a town I had passed through a couple of hours back.

"But surely there's someone here who works on motorcycles," I said. "A shade tree mechanic or something?"

He started to shake his head, and then a mischievous smile spread across his face, and he began tugging at his bolo tie in a manner that seemed to say, "Should I or shouldn't I?"

He finally decided that he should.

"Well, you know," he said, "there *is* a biker bar down the street . . . if you've got the guts to go in there."

I shrugged. "Guts? It's not really a matter of guts. I have to get my bike fixed."

"Okay! Well . . . it's just up the street a couple of blocks. Just ask for Blackie. He owns the place."

"I appreciate it."

I went around to my room, took some of my stuff inside, and then I put on the gnarliest Harley shirt I could find. After I had it on, I did a quick appraisal in the bathroom mirror. I didn't look much like I belonged in a biker bar . . . but maybe the shirt would get me through the door.

It wasn't hard to find the place. The windows were all

boarded up. It didn't look like the warmest, most inviting bar in town, and it was so dark inside that I couldn't see a thing. Gradually, as my eyes became accustomed to the darkness, I could see that the place was packed with biker-types, and they were all staring at me. They knew who the regulars were, and it was apparent right away that I was not a regular.

I launched right in, "My Harley broke down." (I stressed the word "Harley.") No response. "I was told I might get some help here." Still no response. "They said to ask for Blackie?" Nothing.

But I decided to take a chance.

I walked up to the guy sitting behind the bar and stuck out my hand, "You're Blackie, aren't you?"

"Yeah," he said, shaking my hand. "I'm Blackie. What's wrong with your Harley?"

Less than half an hour later, the two of us were standing in his garage, with his tools and pieces of my bike spread out all over the floor. He spent nearly two hours working on it, and it had us both completely baffled. I was surprised by Blackie's willingness to spend so much time helping a complete stranger. That wasn't what I had expected from a guy who ran a biker bar. The only thing that really marked Blackie as a biker was his language. Every other word out of his mouth consisted of four letters, and the swearing increased in intensity and smuttiness as the source of the bike's problems continued to elude us.

"So . . ." he said, finally, "what the . . . . are you doing way the . . . out here anyway. You on vacation or some-thing?"

"No, I do this for a living."

"Really . . . what kind of a . . . . job lets you ride a motorcycle for a living?"

"I'm an evangelist for the Christian Motorcyclists Association."

"What?" The wrench he was holding dropped from his hand and clanked noisily on the garage floor. "Why the . . . . I mean, why didn't you tell me you were a preacher?"

"Why should I?"

"Because I've been cussing."

"Blackie," I said, "I'm not going to judge the way you talk. If you feel comfortable talking that way in front of God, that's between you and Him."

"But I can't see God," he said. "I can see you!"

After Blackie got over his initial shock at hearing that I was an evangelist, he sat down on the floor of his garage and started telling me his life story. He told me about broken relationships, about wrong decisions he had made, and about his biggest worry in life—which was that his only son was following in his footsteps.

"You know . . . I don't have a wife . . . but I've tried to be the best father I know how to be. The problem is, I see that my boy's starting to do the same things I did when I was his age, and I really don't want that to happen. I want him to do something different with his life."

He told me he had sent his son to confirmation classes at one of the local churches, and there were only two weeks more of those. They didn't seem to be doing much good.

"Blackie," I said, "confirmation classes are fine . . . but your boy is like any other boy. He wants to walk in his daddy's footsteps. It's really important that those footsteps take him in the right direction."

I wasn't able to get any further than that. All I could do that day was plant the seeds of the Gospel. But what was interesting was that, no sooner had I done that than I found the problem with my bike. There was a cut cable. It looked, in fact, like it had been sliced through with a razor blade. It took twenty minutes and an expenditure of sixty cents to fix it. And I believe with all my heart that an angel clipped that thing just so I could spend some time with Blackie. That's the only way it made sense. I had ridden more than 100 miles since my last stop, and the bike had started giving me trouble all of a sudden when I got to this little town. I didn't see any way that was possible except through supernatural intervention. How ever I looked at it, it seemed obvious that God had brought me here.

After we fixed the bike, Blackie asked, "Why don't you stay with me tonight?"

"I would," I said, "but I've already paid for a motel room, and it would be wasting money if I didn't use it."

"Well, then, come on back to the bar for awhile. Everyone will want to meet you."

I laughed, "No one wants to meet me."

"Oh, yes, they will," he said emphatically. "Herbie, we see your colors everywhere. People want to talk to you, but to be honest, we're scared of you."

I laughed again. "You're scared of us? I can tell you what scared is! Try walking into a biker bar like yours when you're a stranger in town, and you know you won't exactly fit in. *That's* scared!"

"Herbie, I'm telling you, anybody who's got the guts to wear the colors of CMA . . . we want to hear what they have to say."

"Well, if you're sure."

"Of course I'm . . . . I mean, it would be great."

And so for the rest of that evening—long into the night—I sat on the edge of a pool table in that biker bar, sharing with Blackie and his friends why I did what I did, telling them all about what the Lord meant to me. It was almost like children's church. These tough guy bikers were full of questions. They weren't belligerent or sarcastic. They seemed genuinely interested in hearing what I had to say about God. I spent several hours with them, and it was a great experience.

When the time finally came for me to get back on the road, Blackie gave me a bear hug to say goodbye, and several of the other guys came out to see me off. Nobody had been saved, but I felt good because I knew the seeds had been planted. Blackie slapped me on the back and said that he hoped he'd see me again. I assured him that he would.

During the next few years, my travels took me back through Blackie's town several times. I always stopped to see him, and he always welcomed me as if I were a long lost friend.

Meanwhile, Mom's health continued to deteriorate. She rode with my dad for awhile after her illness was diagnosed, but even when she got to the point where she could no longer sit on a motorcycle, they still traveled the country in their motor home. One time, she literally demanded that we tie her to a motorcycle so she could ride in a parade. That's how important CMA was to her, and particularly the people of CMA.

One of my mother's favorite events was the "Changing of the Colors" rally that is held in the Hatfield area every fall when the leaves are changing colors in the Ouachita Mountains. She went gradually from cane to walker to wheelchair to one of those little electric scooters. But even after she had been forced to take to her bed for good, she asked us to take her to the rally in the motor home so she could be with the people she loved so much.

Those were agonizing days for Dad. He was torn apart inside watching the woman he loved being battered and beaten by a terrible disease. He had cut back significantly from his traveling to be with Mom as much as possible. He felt, correctly, that he needed to be with her. But in being off the road, he was away from the people he loved so much. His pain was multiplied by the fact that he was cut off from personal contact with the people whose support, prayers and companionship were so essential. He was sustained during those difficult days by his love for and trust in Jesus, but he went through some very long and difficult days and nights.

As for Mom, I think I had always known she was an amazing woman, but she really showed her strength, courage and grace to me during the time of her illness.

As multiple sclerosis robbed her of her ability to walk, it also took away her speech and her eyesight. But even as her body began to fail in every way, she did her best to maintain a positive outlook. Her attitude was that the Lord had spared her from cancer. He had given her many more good years than she expected to have. She had seen Kelly and me grow up. She had been able to get to know her grandchildren, and she was grateful for everything God had given her.

If I was amazed by her grace and courage during this time, I was also amazed by her fighting spirit. On two different occasions, her doctor gave her less than six months to live. But as she continued to fight, those months stretched into years.

About once a year during this time, I had the opportunity to stop by and see Blackie. Whenever I did, I tried to talk to him about his need for Jesus, and he was always polite, but it never went any further than that.

One year, I was surprised to find that he had sold the bar. He took me to lunch at a little cafe, and told me that he was trying hard to live a good life.

"I don't know if you know this or not," he said, "but I

haven't had a drink since that night we talked in my garage. What was that? Five years ago now?"

"Something like that," I said. "And I think that's terrific. Congratulations."

"Well," he laughed. "It hasn't been easy. You know, I used to get so thirsty for alcohol that my skin would crawl. My whole body needed it . . . like a fix. That's how much I craved it. But I decided that night that it wasn't taking me where I wanted to go. So, I quit."

I could hardly believe, looking across at him, that he was the same man I had met in that biker bar that night so long ago. He had changed tremendously for the better, and I was glad. But I was also sad that he still didn't understand his need for Jesus.

Blackie didn't know it, but by this time I had friends all over the country praying for his salvation. I wasn't going to give up . . . and there was no way he was going to get away.

During the summer of 1994, I stopped to see him again.

We sat in his shop, talking about what was going on in his life, and how proud he was of the way his son had turned out.

Finally, I said, "You know, Blackie, it's possible that I'll never come through here again. I may never see you again. And if I don't, I want to know something. When I get to heaven, are you going to be there?"

"Sure I am!"

"How do you know?"

He looked hurt. "Oh, come on. You know I'm a good guy. I helped you when you broke down . . . and I've probably helped at least 100 other people, too. I sold the bar. I quit drinking . . . ."

I put up my hand to stop him.

"Blackie," I said, "you *are* a good man. You're one of the best men I know, and you're a true friend."

I shook my head, "But if you've never prayed, in simple child-like faith and asked Jesus to be your Savior, then it doesn't matter how good you've been. It isn't good enough."

He looked as if he had heard me for the first time. "Well . . . how do you do that?"

"It's going to sound simple, but it all boils down to a prayer."

He swallowed hard.

"Herbie," he said. "I'm ready. Let's do it."

Sitting there in the back of his shop, he prayed to receive Christ as Lord and Savior. I have seen many people surrender their lives to Jesus, but I have never seen anyone happier about it than my old friend. Tears of joy ran down his face as he fell gently into the arms of Jesus. It was one of the happiest moments of my life, and I shed a few tears of my own.

I knew right then that even if Blackie had been the only one who had ever come to saving faith in Christ during my travels, it would have been more than worth it.

Back home, I found that Mom's condition had deteriorated even further. That, too, was a cause for tears, but of a very different kind.

Shortly after that, I had to take a trip to Europe. While I was there, I prayed fervently that she would live long enough for me to see her one more time. Everywhere I went, I expected to be greeted with a fax telling me that she had died. But Mom kept hanging on.

When I got home, Diane met me at the airport with the news that Mom was so bad she probably wouldn't make it through the night.

"I just hope she's still alive when we get there," she said.

It was already after midnight, and it was nearly a three-hour drive home. When we finally got there, Mom was still holding on, but just barely. Death seemed so very close. It seemed to draw closer with every tick of the clock. But as she had done so many times, she rallied and fooled the doctors.

During the next month, there were many occasions when the family was called to her bedside because her doctors feared that the end had come. But it didn't happen. God was waiting for the perfect time to take her home.

I spent as much of the next month with her as I possibly could, doing my best to let her know how much I loved and cherished her. During that time, we celebrated her 60th birthday.

On September 24, 1994, my mother, Shirley Shreve, lost her fight for life.

Or, to put it more accurately, she entered into eternal life. As the memorial program printed for her funeral said:

"On September 24, 1994, Shirley Shreve took her first steps since 1989—jubilant steps that ran her straight into the arms of Jesus. Even in the sorrowful hours immediately following her passing, her family could smile through their tears at the thought of Shirley running down the streets of gold, skipping stones in the river of life, and meeting her Savior face to face for the first time."

A glorious reunion is coming!

CHAPTER 18

Into the Future

What does the future hold for the Christian Motorcyclists Association?

Who knows for sure? Only God. We know what we hope to do, but we also know that it's all in God's hands, and that means not only that the future is going to be absolutely glorious, but that it's going to be full of wonderful surprises, too. And to think, it all started with a fist-fight between a rebellious son and his father! You never know what God is going to do.

For example, I remember what happened one time when we were asked to kick off some national motorcycle races with a prayer and a brief devotion. The guy who was supposed to offer the prayer thought it would be a good idea to have some music first, and so he said, "Before I pray, I'd just like to play a song for you." He put in a tape with our version of *God's Not Dead*, and as the song came blasting across the stands, it kicked off a hand-clapping, foot-stomping celebration. Well, guess what. That tape got stuck in the player. And so, all day long they couldn't play anything else.

The normal practice is to play loud rock music between every race—much of it pretty ungodly stuff—but on that particular day, all they could play, over and over and over was our song with its lyrics confirming the existence and loving nature of God.

So, like I said, you never know what God will do. All you can do is sit back and enjoy it when it comes!

Another exciting component of CMA's future is that, with the Lord's help, our work will be spreading all over the world.

We have already had people from a number of other countries come in and talk to us about what we've done, so they could learn how to do something similar in their own countries. We've had groups from Switzerland, South Africa, Zimbabwe. And already there are branches of CMA in Canada, Zimbabwe, Australia, South Africa and several other countries. For that reason we have established the CMA Coalition, which says that if these other groups wish to use the CMA name and logo, then their purposes, priorities and standards have to be up to a certain level. We have no interest in controlling these other groups, but if they identify with us, we want to make sure they share our purposes.

It was my privilege to visit with group members in South Africa recently, and I was amazed by the impact they are having in their country. The presidents of companies like Honda, Suzuki and BMW took the time to meet with me, they considered it that important. The CMA of South Africa hosts a biker breakfast every year, and tickets go for a premium price. It is the motorcycle event of the year for South Africa and is always sold out well in advance, even though it's held in a huge stadium.

What's more, two of South Africa's leading motorcycle racers are active in CMA, and they told the leaders of their government that if they were sent to the United States to go through a Motorcycle Safety Training Program here, they would bring it back home and oversee it through the offices of CMA. And so now, every person in South Africa who gets a motorcycle license has to go through a program sponsored and conducted by the Christian Motorcyclists Association.

These are the types of things that are happening as we go forward in the name of Christ.

Although Dad and the directors had appointed me as the president of CMA several years earlier so he could stay with Mother, at the 1994 Changing of the Colors Rally, he officially presented his vest and colors to me, symbolic of passing on the mantle of his leadership.

As Dad was making this presentation, a solemn seriousness overwhelmed me, and I committed to him, to the Lord, to myself, and to all of CMA to continue this ministry in the same spirit and focus with which he had always led it.

That means that we will continue:

1) To focus on evangelism—as servants, through love, building relationships by going to where the people are.

2) To keep the same focus and spirit of integrity. What this means is that:

- There will be no offerings.
- We will not go into debt.
- There will be no evangelistic "beg letters" sent out by a marketing firm using carnal methods, and written by someone who has never ridden a motorcycle or reached out to the hurting in the name of Jesus.
- We will continue to pray for the Lord to bless CMAers and move their hearts to finance the ministry so we can continue to reach out to the hurting in the highways and byways.
- We will trust the Spirit of God to continue taking CMA forward as a movement, not as a monument to past victories.
- Our mission is people.

CMA started as one man on a bike went out by faith to share Jesus with those who would listen. That same spirit must continue in each of our hearts as it is now multiplied by tens of thousands.

As I conclude this "story of CMA," I want to say that I cannot tell you how a man could die on a cross 2,000 years ago and it could make a difference in my life today. But I know that that event has made a difference—a tremendous difference. In the same way, I don't really know what happens when I push the starter button on my motorcycle and it roars to life. I don't know how it works, but I know that it does. I don't know how a brown cow can eat green grass and give white milk, but I know that it happens.

And I know that Jesus has changed my life . . . and He can change yours, too.

In the opening pages of this book, I told you about a young man I met at a roadside park somewhere in Tennessee. By the grace of God, I was able to lead that young man to saving faith in Jesus Christ. I'm not saying that all of his problems immediately vanished when he accepted Christ as his Lord and Savior. Of course not. But now that young man knows that life has a purpose. He knows he's not alone. He knows that God loves him, so much that He sent His only Son into the world to die for him. And he knows that he will live forever in heaven with God.

CMA members have had untold thousands of encounters like the one I had with that young man. Through those encounters, thousands of men and women have turned to the Lord. Thousands of others have turned and walked away, or angrily told us to leave them alone. But even then, the seeds have been planted. And, really, it wouldn't change what we do if everyone we talked to turned and walked away. We'd still keep on telling them that God loves them. We'd continue riding up and down the highways and byways, taking the good news of salvation to the lost and lonely bikers of America. The love of God compels us.

And that same love makes it impossible for me to close this book without asking a very important question: What about you? Do you know how much God loves you? Have you ever surrendered to His love? If not, I urge you to do it right now . . . wherever you area.

I couldn't begin to count the times I've preached my favorite passage from the Bible. That's John 3:16: "For God so loved the world that he gave his one and only Son, that whoever believes in him shall not perish but have eternal life."

Christ came to save the world. Everyone in the world. That means me, and that means you.

The Bible also tells us that "While we were still sinners, Christ died for us" (Romans 5:8). If you're a sinner, then Christ died for you. And you know what? The Bible tells us in Romans 3:23 that we are *all* sinners.

It's possible that you've come to the end of this book . . . that you've read all about the great things God has done in and through CMA, but you still don't know Him in a personal way. If you don't know God . . . if you've never surrendered your life to Jesus Christ . . . won't you please do it now? It's such an easy thing to do . . . but it has such tremendous significance, not only now, but for all eternity.

All you have to do is pray a simple prayer like this one, believing in your heart that Jesus gave his life to pay the penalty for your sin, and that He rose again on the third day.

"Heavenly Father. Thank you so much for the gift of your Son. Thank you for loving me so much that you sent Him to die in my place. Father, I accept the sacrifice He made on my behalf. In His name, I turn away from my sins, and I ask you to accept me into your family. I surrender my life to Jesus. I accept Him as my Lord and my Savior. Wash me clean, by His blood and in His name. For it is in His name I pray . . . the name of the Lord Jesus Christ. Amen."

If you've prayed that prayer, please write and let me know. I want to hear from you!

May God bless you! And, in the meantime, I'll see you out there . . . on the road!